Women of the
Caribbean

This book should serve a useful purpose both for people interested in women of the Caribbean, and Caribbeaners who wish to explore in greater depth the issues which affect women of the area. It is written by Caribbean women who have done authentic study of areas such as: The Employment of Women, Women and the Act, Women's Economic Contribution to Caribbean Society and Women's Role in the Family.

The introduction by Pat Ellis is a comprehensive overview. It sets the scene for the articles included in the body of the material. She has a first-hand knowledge of many of the subject areas treated by individual authors. This contributed to her ability to be selective in her choice of the most valuable material to be included.

I look forward to the publication of this book as a very useful contribution to the all too limited literature by Caribbean women about Caribbean women.

It should dispel some of the myths which exist and provide authentic information from the point of view of women of the region rather than from that of persons from outside the area whose viewpoint would of necessity be from a different perspective.

Dame Nita Barrow
September 25, 1985

9.95

Women of the Caribbean

edited by
Pat Ellis

Zed Books Ltd.
London and New Jersey

Women of the Caribbean was first published by
Zed Books Ltd., 57 Caledonian Road, London N1 9BU, UK,
and 171 First Avenue, Atlantic Highlands, New Jersey 07716,
USA, in 1986.

Edition for Jamaica published by Kingston Publishers Limited,
1A Norwood Avenue, Kingston 5, Jamaica.

Cover designed by Lee Robinson
Printed and bound in the UK
at The Bath Press, Avon.

British Library Cataloguing in Publication Data

Ellis, Pat
    Women of the Caribbean.
    1. Women—Caribbean Area—
    Social conditions
    I. Title
    305.4'2'091821   HQ1501

    ISBN 0-86232-596-X
    ISBN 0-86232-597-8 Pbk

Jamaican ISBN 976-625-011-1

Contents

To my children

**Jacqueline, Suzanne, Pauline,
Peter and Gordon**

and

For all Caribbean Women

Acknowledgements

Over the last ten years there has been a sharp increase in the amount written about Caribbean women; and much of this output has been by Caribbean women themselves.

Facts, views and opinions have been expressed in research reports, articles in academic journals, newspapers and magazines as well as in literary works—short stories, poems and plays. These have attempted to understand Caribbean women more fully, to give expression to their fears, hopes, aspirations, frustrations and triumphs and to highlight their perceptions of themselves.

The writing is scattered throughout the region; but much of it is in special journals and publications in University libraries and/or in special resource centres, such as the Women and Development Unit of the Extra-Mural Department, University of the West Indies, Barbados (WAND). It is therefore accessible only to a relatively small audience.

The aim of this collection is to bring together in one volume a small part of this written material, to present it in simple, readable form and make it available to a wider audience. It was inspired by the WAND series "Issues Concerning Women and Development. A series of articles to stimulate Discussion and Debate in the Caribbean". Nine of the articles* are edited versions of these papers. The introduction and six other articles* were especially written for this collection. Other articles are included by permission of the authors.

This collection has been completed with the assistance and cooperation of many people; it would be impossible to identify them all here by name. Some, however, do deserve special mention.

Special thanks and appreciation to WAND for permission to use selected "Issues" papers and other material from its resource centre—including photographs and the list of resource material in Appendix II. To the Unit's secretarial and library staff, my thanks for their willing assistance and for responding so cheerfully to my numerous queries and requests for information.

To Annette, Sonia, Hannah and Franklin, thanks for valuable ideas and

*Marked in the table of contents

suggestions during the early stages of thinking through the project.

To Norma, Jeanette, Peggy and Beryl, whose discussions helped me to sharpen woolly thinking and clarify ideas for the introduction and whose advice, moral support and encouragement throughout spurred me on—much thanks.

Thanks to Veronica, Joyce and Florence for typing the first draft of the manuscript.

To the contributors who so willingly gave me permission to edit and use their work and without whose confidence in me there would be no book—my gratitude.

My thanks too to those sensitive and committed Caribbean men—Austin, Ben, David, Edward, Egbert, George, Henry, Ronnie and Massy, among others—with whom I have been fortunate to work and to exchange ideas on women's issues. By their attitudes and commitment, they have reinforced my belief—and that of many other Caribbean women—that the barriers between the sexes can be broken down if and when women and men mutually respect each other, enter into dialogue and work together to achieve common goals.

Finally, to Caribbean women from all walks of life who without knowing it, by their example, their love and support have been the motivation for this venture and have made the effort worthwhile.

Any omissions or other shortcomings are mine.

Pat Ellis

Introduction—An Overview of Women in Caribbean Society

by Pat Ellis

Images of Caribbean Women

The image of the strong, independent and dominant Caribbean woman is a familiar one. But what is less well known or understood are the factors that have made her this way and how her society uses them to discriminate against her in both overt and subtle ways.

In rapidly changing Caribbean society, Caribbean women experience many problems and face situations that constantly challenge and undermine their independence. To overcome this, they, like their mothers before them, draw on their strength and resourcefulness, devising unique strategies to overcome the obstacles that threaten to curtail their freedom.

Like most people in poor developing countries, women and men in the English-speaking Caribbean are struggling towards self-sufficiency. Living in societies with few natural or financial resources, they face the problems of poverty and unemployment, of dependency on industrialized countries and of being part of an International Economic Order in which the odds are heavily stacked against them.

Several other factors have contributed to the present position of Caribbean women: the historical heritage of economic and political dependence on England during the periods of slavery and colonialism; increasing North American influence in the post-independence decades (1960s-80s) and the unique Creole culture of Caribbean society. Their situations, the problems that they face, the issues that concern them; and their achievements, must all be seen not only within the social, political and economic realities of the region, but in relation to Caribbean men.

Although the lives of women in different parts of the region do not differ greatly, Caribbean women are not a homogenous group. Divisions of race, colour, class, social and economic status and place of residence affect their lives and are responsible for significant differences in their perceptions of themselves, their role and their contributions to the development of their countries. Perhaps this is why many Caribbean women perceive themselves and their status more in terms of education and work opportunities and the effects of adverse social and economic conditions than in terms of inequality.

The majority of women are black, either of African descent or of mixed

1

race. In Guyana and Trinidad approximately 40% of the population is of East Indian descent. In every island there are small numbers of local whites— descendants of various European colonials—as well as expatriate whites who have settled in recent years. Women of this group form a small minority and since little research has been done on them, little is known about their perceptions of themselves in relation to the rest of the society, or of the contradictions and conflicts with which they have been confronted, especially during the last two decades. Even smaller ethnic groups of Chinese, Syrians and Portuguese exist, as do very small pockets of native Amerindians in Guyana, Dominica and St Vincent. As with the white and East Indian women, very little is known about the lives, perceptions and specific concerns of women in these (minority) groups.

In recent years, and especially since International Women's Year in 1975, there has been a tremendous increase in interest among women themselves, among national planners and among the wider population in all aspects of the lives of Caribbean women. A significant amount of research and investigation has been and still is taking place on various aspects of women's lives and most of this has focused on the many mainly black women in rural communities. These women are at the bottom of the socio-economic ladder and have fewer opportunities than their sisters in the middle and upper classes. But although the latter have more opportunities to acquire professional, executive and administrative positions of their choice, many women from the lower class have been able to attain social mobility through education, have become teachers and nurses, and have gone into commerce and the public (civil) service.

Changing Roles and Responsibilities of Women

Caribbean women, like their counterparts in other parts of the world, are struggling for real freedom and equality. In their efforts to achieve this they are subjected to a great deal of tension and frustration. At the same time, the participation of women at all levels of Caribbean society, their initiative and success, is beginning to be publicly recognized by legislation and programmes aimed at alleviating their special problems.

In recent years many more women from all classes and ethnic groups have been able to move successfully into non-traditional areas of activity, in some cases they have gained improved status and greater respect—as well as financial rewards. A few women have managed to reach the top of their professions and attain powerful positions in their countries; many more are aspiring to do so. There has been a significant increase in the number of women in the teaching and nursing professions, while many professional women hold responsible, senior positions in the public and private sectors. A small handful of Caribbean women have distinguished themselves in the international arena and hold important posts in international agencies such as the UN. Such women are valuable as role models for other women in the society.

But the small number of such visible women and the growing number who are penetrating the higher echelons of administration and policy-making are only a fraction of the two-and-a-half million women in the region. Many more women need to be encouraged to develop their full potential, to enter into the non-traditional fields of business, science and technology. There is still a general disinclination for—and some strong resistance to—changes in the role and status of women. This unwillingness to accept change is not only exhibited by men but by some women themselves. On the other hand, there are many committed women and men in the region who are working to ensure that Caribbean women are given the recognition and benefits commensurate with the important contributions that they are making in all areas to the development of their countries.

Efforts to reorient the education of women and to eliminate sex stereotyping in school curricula have begun. They must be considerably speeded up if education is not to continue to reinforce the inequalities of career options between girls and boys, and if the prevailing attitudes of society are not to continue to force women to conform to the traditional roles. Many people—both men and women—still find it difficult to accept women in non-traditional roles and to accept the inevitable changes in the roles and responsibilities of men and women that follow.

Women's Economic Role

The majority of Caribbean women have always been—and still are—engaged in a variety of economic activities outside the home. Yet very little attention has been paid to the vital contribution that they make to the economies of the various countries in the region. Economic analyses of the character and problems of Caribbean economies have consistently ignored the ways in which women participate in economic activity in the formal and informal sectors, the problems that they face as they do so, or the ways in which their contributions in these sectors affect the entire economy.

Women and Work
As slaves and the descendants of slaves the majority of Caribbean women are accustomed to working outside the home for financial returns. Women work for economic survival. They have always had a major responsibility for providing for the care and nurturing of their family, as well as the economic responsibility of satisfying basic needs. They could not depend on their husbands or male partners for financial support since the latter's position in the poor lower strata of the society did not provide them with the means to provide adequate financial support for a wife and family. Work is not only natural, it as an integral part of their experience, their lives and their self-image. A long history of work has given them access to money and a sense of independence. It has broadened their social relationships beyond the home, increased their self-esteem and given them considerable power within their

3

families and communities. Working women make a substantial contribution to Caribbean economies, both as wage-earners in the formal public and private sector and as small entrepreneurs in the informal sector.

Women have been a vital source of cheap unskilled/semi-skilled labour. First during slavery as field and house slaves, as labourers on the plantations and estates after emancipation, and in the post-independence period as workers in the new industries and factories. Towards the end of the period of slavery, when slaves were given a small piece of land to plant their own provisions, women began to sell their surplus produce on Saturdays to earn money independently. This was the beginning of the higgler/hawker/huckster trade in internal markets and is still an important economic activity for many women in the lower echelons of contemporary Caribbean society. Although not fully recognized as such, this internal and regional market system is a vital part of the region's economy.

Women have always predominated in the traditional and informal sectors of the economy and they are still more likely than men to work there. Female higglers have higher status than men in the market-place. In Jamaica a successful male higgler is said to "act like a woman" and an unsuccessful one is said "not to know how to act like a woman". But within the larger society higglering is viewed as a low status job.

Women in Agriculture

In the predominantly agricultural economy of the region, a great deal depends on the labour of rural black and East Indian (in Trinidad and Guyana) women. Women forty-years-old and over form a high percentage of the agricultural labour force. They work for long hours, for low pay and perform a wide variety of tasks. They not only produce the bulk of the food in the region, they sort, pack, transport, process and distribute it. As traders, they dominate the domestic and regional markets' trade in fruits, vegetables, root crops and fish. Over the years they have perfected simple methods of food processing and make large quantities of jams, jellies and other preserves for home consumption and for sale. Many women cultivate kitchen-gardens on small plots adjoining their houses. Women in agriculture and female farmers generally face many problems and endure many hardships. Apart from low wages, seasonal work, lack of access to agricultural information and technology and few opportunities for training, these women lack access to the resources of land, equipment and credit. An increase in their work-load, therefore, does not necessarily bring increased returns. For female traders, lack of market information and of organized cooperative ventures, competition from imported goods and lack of legal status or protection undermine the profit they can make from their ventures. For farmers and traders, "invisibility" and the exclusion of their contribution from national statistics have continued to keep planners in the region from recognizing and acknowledging the vital role that they play in the economy.

In recent years some attempt to address this issue has been made in the national agricultural plans of some countries. At the same time, more women are becoming qualified as agronomists, food technologists and extension workers. This should not only increase the flow of relevant information to female farmers and traders, but lead to an increased sensitivity which will ensure that their concerns and problems are channelled to and dealt with at the highest level of decision-making.

Women in Industry

During the late 1960s and 1970s, many governments invited foreign companies to set up offshore manufacturing operations in Caribbean countries in an attempt to stimulate economic growth in the region. Promises of tax concessions, a steady supply of cheap unskilled and semi-skilled labour, low wages and the absence of strict adequate legislation to control operations have resulted in the establishment of a significant number of export-oriented industries—mainly electronics and textiles—in several countries in the region. With the growth of this manufacturing sector many young women moving from the rural communities into the urban areas to seek employment have found jobs in these new industries. This has not only depleted the agricultural sector of younger workers, but has paved the way for these women to be exploited on a large and organized scale.

Large factory shells have been built in which women work in cramped conditions with insufficient light and air and with inadequate toilet and recreational facilities. In the factories the women work for very low wages and receive few benefits. Their jobs are insecure and they live in constant fear of losing them. On the whole they are not encouraged to join unions and in some cases are actually prohibited from so doing within the terms of agreement between the government and the parent company (usually USA-based). They therefore have little or no protection against various types of exploitation, including sexual harassment. In many cases workers are forced to serve an apprenticeship period which may last as long as six months. During this time they receive half-pay and can be fired without notice. Many women in these factories are hired on temporary contracts.

The work that they do is often monotonous and repetitive piece-work and the competition is fierce as the price per piece can be as low as 25 cents. It often requires sitting or standing for long hours operating faulty machinery or doing fine handiwork such as embroidery. The women's health is often endangered, especially in the electronics industries where they work with chemicals without protective clothing. In these cases no attempt is made to educate the women about the dangers to which they are being exposed and many experience eye strain, skin problems, dizziness, headaches and backaches. Since in most of these situations women are not entitled to sick-leave or holidays they can easily be dismissed.

There is also little opportunity for women to move up into managerial or administrative posts within these factories. The managers are usually men who, because of their perceptions about the biological and psychological characteristics of women, have very traditional and rigid ideas about the roles that women should play. Many of these managers express the view that women are more suited to the tedious and montonous work in the factories than men. Most agree that men would not remain in such dull work for long. Many say that in their opinion women have more manual dexterity, are accustomed to fine work such as sewing and are *willing to settle for low wages* while *men as the breadwinners* are not.

The belief that women's income is supplementary to that of men still persists. In fact, many of the women employed in these industries are solely responsible for the financial support of their families and *that* is why they accept the low wage which is better than no wage. This exploitation of large numbers of women within the manufacturing and industrial sector is not peculiar to the Caribbean. It is part of a larger phenomenon of the exporting of "undesirable" jobs and off-shore sourcing in the poor, developing countries in Asia, Latin America and the Caribbean, mainly by large transnational corporations in the USA.

Labour Force Participation

Women are approximately 40% of the labour force. Over the last decade or so, with the growth of the public and private sectors, the manufacturing sector and tourism, the textile industry and enclave electronic industries, there has been an increase in the numbers of women employed in the formal sectors of the economy. But the majority of women are concentrated within the service sectors. In the smaller islands women form approximately 66% of all service workers while in the region as a whole the figure is 53%.

Governments are the major employers in the formal sector. The percentage of women employed by governments ranges from 22-28% in most countries in the region. By and large women are in traditional female occupations and are concentrated in the fields of education, nursing and social work; a significant number are employed in domestic service as home-helps and many others are self-employed as seamstresses, hairdressers and petty traders.

It is only very recently that there has been an increase in the numbers of women in previously male-dominated areas of employment and at the highest levels of decision-making in the private and public sector. In every country in the region there are now women in senior management and administrative positions in both the private and public sectors. The appointment of women as permanent secretaries, as ministers of religion and of government, as presidents and chairpersons of businesses and statutory bodies and the inroads made by female engineers, welders and masons into previously male-dominated areas reflect the slowly changing patterns of participation within the labour force.

The small number of women who have reached the top in their professions and are in powerful positions, and the steadily increasing number who are moving up into important managerial and administrative positions have been able to do so through hard work and determination, often against tremendous odds. But they are still in the minority and the majority of women continue in the lower paid, lower status, jobs, and it should be emphasized that more women than men are to be found in the lowest paid jobs.

Large numbers of women, rural and urban, from all classes and ethnic groups, are actively engaged in a wide variety of small economic enterprises and income-earning activities. Most of these women see themselves and are seen by society as housewives; they are therefore not recorded in the official labour force statistics. In recent years, however, more attention is being focused on this informal sector and on the participation of women within it. This in turn has raised the question of the need for more precise data and the use of new and alternative research instruments to collect and record this vital aspect of women's work. Planners and policy-makers are being forced to recognize the serious implications for national development planning if the contribution of these women continues to remain invisible.

The Family

Family forms in the Caribbean are very diverse. The European concept of the nuclear family with its ideology of patriarchy and male dominance, the women-centred matriarchial type and the extended family type, legacies from African and East Indian cultures respectively, all exist simultaneously in the region. Single parent families and female-headed households are realities for many women at all levels of Caribbean society. Family members do not all necessarily reside in the same household, and the concept of family often goes beyond blood relations and kin to include close friends and neighbours.

A variety of mating patterns and unions exist. Legal marriage, common-law unions and visiting relationships* all exist; but on the whole the institution of marriage is still seen to be the most desirable union. High social value is placed on it and young women continue to be pressured both covertly and overtly into marriage. The highest proportion of marital unions are in Trinidad, Guyana and Belize—countries with significant East Indian populations.

For many older women and couples in the lower socio-economic bracket, marriage has been equated with improved socio-economic status and in many cases couples have lived for years in common-law unions until they have saved enough money to afford a wedding. Now younger women of this group, while having marriage as a long term goal, are usually involved in some type of visiting relationship. Within recent years many middle-class young women are questioning the institution of marriage and are experimenting with a variety of alternatives such as single parenting or visiting relationships; many are rejecting the idea of marriage as the ultimate goal.

---

* Meaning a semi-permanent relationship in which the man does not live in the same household as the woman but visits from time to time. The regularity and duration of such visits varies.

Male-Female Relationships

Within society attitudes to male-female relationships and to marriage are ambivalent and contradictory. On the one hand girls are taught from an early age strategies to ensure their survival and that of their families whether a male is present or not. This creates a sense of independence—hence the image of the strong Caribbean women who can cope with anything. At the same time they are also taught that it is not only desirable, but important, to have a male partner; that in the male-female relationship the man is dominant and that the woman is not free to do as she wishes but must defer to her mate. On the other hand, the belief that getting married gives women added responsibility, status and independence is often captured in the phase "now that you are married you are your own woman."

Young men receive similarly contradictory messages. By and large boys are not socialized and taught survival skills and strategies in the way that girls are. In the absence of this they depend very heavily on their mothers, other female relatives and later on their wives and partners. However, because they too have internalized the ideology of male dominance, deep down they resent their dependence on their strong female counterparts. These feelings of resentment are often carried over into their adult relationships and can lead to tension and hostility as Caribbean men and women play out their conflicting roles and expectations of each other. Children see their strong dominant mothers experiencing oppression and showing insecurity as they relate to their male partners and this cycle continues and repeats itself in the next generation. These double standards and ambivalent attitudes inevitably affect the self-image and sense of worth of Caribbean women.

Violence

Violence against women and children occurs in a significant number of families, not only in the lower echelons of society where it is often more overt and direct, but within the middle and upper classes as well. Here, the physical and psychological violence against women is perhaps more subtle and although just as severe has been less acknowledged. Attitudes previously reinforced the societal belief that violence in the family was a private matter between man and woman and that outsiders should not interfere. The shame, guilt and stigma attached to wife-beating, sexual harassment and rape usually prevented female victims from openly admitting to being a victim. In recent years, however, the problem has been brought more into the open and there is a growing realization that wife-beating, incest and rape are not isolated phenomena confined to lower-class women, but that women and girls of all ages and classes are being subjected to this type of violence daily.

In the Caribbean, as in other parts of the world, strategies to deal with violence against women within the law are either non-existent or grossly inadequate. Although rape, wife-beating, assault and incest are crimes punishable by law, it is very difficult for the victims to prove their innocence. Many men, including law enforcement officers, police and judges firmly believe that women "ask for it", "like it" or "deserve it". There are men who have so internalized the ideology of male dominance that they believe and act as if it is their right to use violence to control and keep women in submission.

In most countries of the region there are no formal mechanisms outside the law through which problems of violence against women can be dealt with. Half-way houses, homes for battered women, rape crisis centres and counselling services are virtually non-existent. Women continue to rely on the sympathetic understanding of female relatives and friends. More attention has recently begun to be paid to the problems of violence against women, mainly as a result of the initiatives of non-governmental organizations (NGOs). In Trinidad concerned women's groups have organized seminars on this issue and have promoted wide media coverage to focus attention on the sharp increase in the number and variety of sexual crimes against women. In Jamaica an activist women's group (Sistren) recently conducted research on the issue by interviewing victims of sexual violence. The publication *Say No to Sexual Violence* in which the findings have been presented not only provides information on the increase in the number and severity of sexual crimes, but gives insights into the indignities to which women are exposed if they attempt to seek redress through the law. In Jamaica within the last few months a small Rape Crisis Centre has been set up to provide information, counselling services and legal advice to women. A similar centre has recently been set up in Trinidad.

There is no doubt that more women have begun to talk out against the violence, indignities and injustices that they suffer at the hands of men. But there are still large numbers of women who are constantly exposed to physical and psychological violence. Most of these women feel powerless to cope to remove themselves from the situation. For some their economic or psychological dependence on men keep them there; for others it is the lack of alternatives, or the belief that there are none, that prevents their escape.

Motherhood

High value and status is attached to the mothering role. Women are expected to bear children and childless women are often looked down upon. Caribbean women of all classes and races, irrespective of marital status, accept responsibility for child-care and child rearing. Although full-time mothering and house-minding might at one time have been seen to be the ideal, it has never been the norm. In the 1950s and 1960s it was regarded as a status symbol and a matter of prestige for the man who could afford it to have a non-working wife or partner.

The great importance attached to motherhood has provided women with considerable influence, authority and respect. Seventy-five percent of all Caribbean women are mothers and the average number of children per mother is 4.5. For many women, having children is seen as an economic investment for their old age and on the whole women start bearing children from an early age. There is a high proportion of teenage pregnancies and this can put a premature end to the education of young women, since they usually have to leave school when they become pregnant. In Jamaica a women's centre was established in 1978 offering programmes for adolescent mothers; many young women have been given the opportunity to continue and complete their education during their pregnancy and after the birth of their children. The centre has also been able to involve some of the babies' fathers in their programme of education and counselling. To date 98% of the participants have not had a second pregnancy.

Many women in the region who have had no biological children of their own care for and raise the children of others. Children may be cared for by relatives (grandmothers, aunts), god-mothers or by close friends and neighbours. From the days of slavery Caribbean women have learnt to adapt their family structures to suit their economic situation. Shared mothering releases the biological mother to seek paid employment overseas or in urban centres. It also allows her to make use of opportunities for higher education.

Coping Strategies

Women in the Caribbean are unique in the way that they have explored and adopted strategies for coping and for survival. They are involved in a wide variety of social networks that provide support and function as support systems on which they can draw in time of need. These networks provide economic as well as emotional support. Most urban middle-class women have relatives who own land in rural communities and who can supply them with food, while they will often reciprocate by sending clothing, money and other utilitarian gifts to relatives in rural areas. Kinship, family and neighbourhood networks—especially in rural communities—provide assistance with farming, child-care and housebuilding. This sharing and interdependence not only helps women to cope with their family responsibilities, but act as a buffer in times of emotional stress and strain and economic crisis. Through these networks Caribbean women have developed strong feelings of solidarity.

Religious faith has always been very influential in the lives of women in the region. Women have always played a central role in the indigenous religions as spiritual mothers and sisters and in recent years attempts to have women ordained to the ministry in some of the established churches have been successful. Women have always drawn great strength and support from their faith and continue to do so; but it is noticeable that religious involvement does not appear to have as much significance in the lives of younger women in the region.

Women in Organizations

A recent survey carried out in three islands showed that the majority of women were not members of any formal organizations, but any definition of participation that is focused only on involvement in formally organized groups will fail to capture and consider the many informal groupings, networks and associations in which large numbers of women are involved.

Voluntary Non-Governmental Organizations—NGOs

Women in the region have a history of active involvement in voluntary social groups both at the community and national levels and more increasingly at the regional level. Church groups, mothers' unions, women's leagues, the Women's Federation, groups and associations, mothers' clubs, YWCA, Soroptomists, the Business and Professional Women's Club, Lionesses and professional associations of secretaries and nurses are to be found in every country in the Caribbean. Previously these organizations were not particularly concerned with women's issues and their programmes tended to reinforce and perpetuate the stereotyped role of women as wife and mother. In spite of this they have a history of valuable work in the region; they have been vehicles of self-expression and have had lasting effects on social interaction and community life. They are usually very flexible and operate by and large in non-bureaucratic and non-authoritarian ways. They depend on community leadership and encourage self-reliance. They enjoy the support and trust of community members and as such as they have the potential to be powerful tools for social change and national development.

Historically, these community organisations have been managed by and for women. The majority of the members are women, and their programmes and projects are usually geared to address the problems of women and to improve their social situation; throughout the region there are literally hundreds of these community groups in which thousands of women actively participate. By their involvement in such groups many women have gained valuable experience and have developed their skills in planning, organization, management and leadership; others have improved their skills in child-care, nutrition and interpersonal relationships. Others by their dedication, commitment and vision have served as role models and have motivated their fellow-men and women to high levels of achievement. Such women are held in high esteem and in many cases are recognized as important leading figures in the life and affairs of their communities. But only a relatively small number of these women have been given the recognition at the national level that they so richly deserve.

In many cases these groups and organizations are not provided with much-needed support and resources. They are not always seen as being linked to goals of national development or as being a vital tool in national planning strategies. Because by and large they are regarded as marginal, their existence has continued to keep women outside of the mainstream of development activity. Yet these women's organizations have not consistently sought to influence national policy. Why not? A careful examination of them should be undertaken to provide information and insights into: what kind of structures have been developed? How effective are these? How are they maintained? What type of decision-making process exists? To what extent have women's organizations effected changes in the policy of government, the church, trade unions and the media? Why have women not tried more systematically to bring about change in these institutions which would enhance their positions as

11

active contributors to decision-making and policy formulation?

Within the last decade some of the existing women's organizations which historically were oriented to social welfare have begun to take on a different perspective. Some have begun to reorient their programmes to focus on the position of women and the social and economic constraints with which they are faced. Organizations throughout the region are now implementing more programmes and projects whose aims are to promote greater self confidence and to encourage self-reliance in women at all levels. But although it is clear that many of these NGOs are slowly beginning to reform, very few have taken any radical steps to transform themselves into activist organizations.

During the UN Decade for Women, National Councils or Organizations of Women were formed in some countries in an attempt to coordinate and pool resources of the large number of smaller groups. Their success has varied from country to country. In some they have played a strong role by stimulating debate on women's issues. Some women's groups have begun to put pressure on governments to respond to their demands for greater recognition of women's contribution, for more support and resources for women and women's groups and for the greater involvement of women at all levels of national development.

In these ways women's NGOs are slowly beginning to challenge the dominant structures and systems and forcing those in power to take note of women. By so doing they are contributing to the growing sense of purpose and solidarity among the women in the region.

Political Involvement of Women
In the Caribbean the view is still widely held that opportunities do exist for women to be more fully involved at all levels of society, if only women would make use of them. Women's non-involvement is seen as a deliberate choice; but a closer examination of women's reluctance to accept higher positions opened to them reveals the importance that society has placed on their domestic role. Hesitancy is often due to the increased demands that such positions will make on their time and their family's life. As long as greater importance is placed on women's reproductive role than on their economic and civic roles, women will continue to be excluded from greater involvement at the level of policy- and decision-making. Although women in the Caribbean have a great deal of power in the family, this is seen as secondary to the power of men who operate in public and political spheres; and the positions of power and leadership that large numbers of women occupy within community groups and women's organizations is not reflected by their participation in the political sphere.

All the major political parties in the region boast of a women's arm, women's league or women's auxiliary. However, the head of the party is invariably male, and although there is a female Prime Minister, a few female cabinet ministers, senators and permanent secretaries, there is also a conspicious absence of large numbers of women in party administration, in the houses of parliament or in senior positions within the governments. For instance, in nine territories, of 237 members in the houses of representatives, only 23 (9.7%) are women; of 94 senators only 11 (11.7%) are women, and of 111 cabinet ministers only 5 (4.5%) are women.

Because the women's arms of political parties are branches of the main party, their autonomy and contribution to party policy-making is limited. They do, however, play an important role in campaigning, mobilizing members and raising funds. They have been particularly effective in campaigning at election time and some male candidates say that they prefer the women to campaign because the women do it better and are very highly committed. It is important to note, however, that the women have not been able to use their campaigning skill to secure for themselves a larger number of representatives in positions of power within the party structures. In very many cases there are only one or two token women on the party executive while the majority continue to allow themselves to be used by the men in the party to keep their (the men's) power positions intact.

At the same time, because there is a stigma attached to women who enter politics, many women shy away from actively becoming involved in politics. Those women who do are often ridiculed, discriminated against and exploited not only by men but also by other women. Most women never perceive that they could be leaders or decision-makers at the political level. Within many of the established political parties it is the older women party stalwarts who have been in leadership positions in the women's arms and who by and large have been content to play a traditional supportive role and to toe the party line. This has been the case even within some of the more radical parties; and when some of the younger, more activist women have attempted to get power at the highest level of party policy- and decision-making their attempts have been very firmly curtailed.

Within the last few years, however, a small number of activist women's groups are emerging both within political parties—in the New Jewel Movement—the People's Revolutionary Government of Grenada (1979-85), the Working People's Alliance in Guyana, and outside (Concerned Women for Progress in Jamaica and Trinidad, Sistren theatre collective in Jamaica). It is generally younger women who join these groups; they are more politically aware than their counterparts in the women's arms and their orientation is predominantly socialist and feminist. These groups organize around issues that affect women and their relationship to the existing societal structures and political systems. A large part of their work focuses on raising women's consciousness and mobilizing them to take action that will change the subordinate position that they hold in the society. Such groups, although small and very few in number, are playing a vital role in helping women and the public to begin to understand the *political* implications of women's subordination.

If the inequalities and injustices to which women are subjected are to be tackled effectively, it is women themselves who will have to tackle them at the highest levels. Caribbean women need to harness the power and authority that they have in their families and communities and to translate this into action in the political arena. A small step is being made in this direction as more women in the region are beginning to see the need to mobilize and organize themselves around women's issues.

Participation in Trade Unions

Many women in the region participate in trade unions; like political parties, many trade unions have a women's auxiliary. More women are members of unions than of political parties and female employees in government service and in some private sector industries are members of one or other of the existing unions. They actively participate in union activity and support strike action when necessary. But very few women are usually seriously involved in union negotiations, bargaining or arbitration, and although a few outstanding women have headed large unions (Ursula Gittens of the Civil Service Association and Monica Gopaul of Teachers' Union in Trinidad, Yvonne Francis Gibson of the Teachers' Union in St Vincent), these are the exception rather than the rule. Moreover, very few trade unions have agitated for women's rights or for better conditions of work specifically for their female workers. Any benefits that women have received in this area have resulted from the unions' agitation for improved conditions for all workers—male and female. A small number of unions with all-female membership such as the Housewives' Associations of Trinidad & Tobago (HATT), National Union of Domestic Employees in Trinidad, have agitated successfully for minimum wages and other benefits for women who work in domestic service.

In an attempt to motivate trade union women to take on executive, management and leadership positions within their unions, the Trade Union Institute of the Extra-Mural Department of UWI Mona, Jamaica, implemented a three-year project in 1981. This regional project was coordinated by Marva Philips a prominent Jamaican woman trade unionist. Its main objective was to upgrade the skills and increase the capability of trade union women. Through a number of regional and national workshops women were offered knowledge and skills which could give them the confidence to operate at higher levels in their unions.

The Caribbean Women's Movement (CWM)

Regional Level Initiatives

Caribbean women have for years worked through voluntary groups to improve the welfare of other women. In 1970 a number of prominent women who had had long experience in this field got together and formed the Caribbean Women's Association (CARIWA), an umbrella agency for women's NGOs in the region. This organization stimulated other similar initiatives at regional levels and gave birth to what has become a vibrant Caribbean women's movement. In 1973 the Conference on the Affairs and Status of Women in Guyana (CASWIG) was started as a national counterpart to CARIWA and over the years other national umbrella organizations have been formed by

NGOs in many of the territories. In the early 1970s the women's auxiliary of the Jamaica People's National Party (PNP) and the Women's Revolutionary Socialist Movement (WRSM) of the People's National Congress (PNC) in Guyana were both instrumental, when their parties came into power, in causing the government to set up machinery for the recognition of women as equal partners in national development. By the mid-1970s improving the role and status of women had become one of the objectives of all the territories.

The coming of International Women's Year and of the UN Decade of Women helped Caribbean women to consolidate their earlier initiatives and gave new emphasis and impetus to the women's movement in the region. In 1977, Caribbean women organized a seminar in Jamaica in which representatives of governments, of national and regional women's organizations and of international agencies participated. This meeting produced a Regional Plan of Action for Caribbean Women which was later incorporated into the regional plan of the UN Economic Commission for Latin America. The women at this meeting agreed to establish, within one year, a unit whose function was to implement the plan by developing concrete programmes and projects that would facilitate the greater participation of women in the development of the region. Its focus was to be on women in rural communities in the Windward and Leeward Islands (the Lesser Developed Countries (LDCs)).

The Women and Development Unit (WAND)
This unit, a direct outcome of the 1977 seminar, was set up in 1978 within the Extra-Mural Department—the outreach arm—of the University of the West Indies. It is situated at the Cave Hill Campus in Barbados. During the seven years of its existence, WAND has developed and implemented an extensive and impressive programme and a method of working that has had tremendous impact not only through the region but internationally. The three major aspects of its work has been the raising of awareness about women's issues, the provision of technical assistance to women's groups and to governments in the region, and the development and implementation of experimental pilot projects as models of the what and how of integrating women's concerns with development plans, programmes and projects.

Raising Awareness: WAND has done much to create a climate in the region within which it is possible to discuss women's issues. The Unit produces and disseminates material on and for women through a wide variety of media. The quarterly newsletter *Woman Speak!* is widely circulated throughout the region. There is an ongoing series of articles, 'Issues concerning Women and Development', which are used by groups and organizations as discussion starters. 'Woman Struggle' provides news and information on women from an international perspective. Research studies, monographs and reports about Caribbean women's activities are commissioned and produced and along with similar material on women elsewhere are available in the Unit's documentation and research centre. Training manuals, resource books and audio-visual material, slide-tapes, videos, posters and photographs—produced by the Unit are widely used by groups and agencies—NGO and government alike—throughout the region.

As well as producing and disseminating material, the Unit has an on-going consciousness-raising programme; its staff conduct sensitizing sessions with a variety of groups at various levels in the region. Such sessions are carried out with teachers in training colleges, with students in secondary schools, with extension workers and with senior officers and officials in government ministries, with professional groups, with community and women's groups and with students in various faculties and departments within the university. Through these sessions key groups in each territory are constantly being made aware of the concerns, problems, and needs of women and of the important role they play in development. Other strategies for raising awareness have been the organization of conferences, seminars and workshops at national and regional levels, and special efforts to sensitize men, especially those in influential positions.

Provision of Technical Assistance: The Unit provides technical assistance to women's groups at all levels from community to national and regional and to governmental and other agencies. For the former, assistance has been in the area of identifying resources—financial and otherwise—providing training in project development, technical and management skills and in evaluation. For the latter, assistance has been in providing training, programme planning, research and evaluation, consultation and advisory services.

Pilot Projects: Through the development and implementation of experimental projects, WAND has produced a model that shows how women at the community level can actively participate in research, programme planning and the evaluation of development projects, and how, by using a participatory methodology, projects can be effectively linked to and influence national planning so that the concerns of women are adequately addressed.

In all of its activities WAND has paid special attention to building the capacity and capabilities of local institutions and women's groups. To this end it has consistently collaborated with groups and agencies at national and regional level. In this way it has helped to develop the sense of solidarity among women at all levels of Caribbean society.

Caricom Women's Desk

In 1980 the Caribbean Community Secretariat (CARICOM) appointed a women's affairs adviser who later became the Women's Affairs Officer of the Secretariat. The Desk has been instrumental not only in supporting programmes for women at the national level, but has played a critical role in helping to promote and strengthen machinery for women at the governmental level. It has provided the various women's desks, bureaux and departments with resources, technical assistance and training, and has collaborated with CARIWA and WAND to facilitate similar activities.

The Desk, as the regional governmental machinery, has been able to provide a forum at which the concerns of Caribbean women can be discussed at the highest level. This forum came into being in March 1981 with the first meeting of Ministers Responsible for Integration of Women in Development. Similar meetings followed in 1983 and 1985. At these meetings, ministers are briefed and provided with relevant information on women relating to the various sectors of the national economy. Plans are then developed for the implementation of policies at national level. The Desk has also introduced women's issues and concerns into other similar fora, and at other ministerial meetings such as agriculture and health. Women's issues specific to these sectors are presented via briefing notes and background documents to each minister or department. In this way the Desk has been able to sensitize and keep the governments' policy-makers and planners informed and to impress upon them the importance of women to national and regional development.

National Initiatives

Encouraged and supported by events and activities at the regional level as well as by the thrust of International Women's Year and the UN Decade, the number of initiatives in individual territories increased rapidly between 1975 and 1985. Many women's groups and NGOs began to play a greater role and to agitate for more recognition for women. They organized national conferences, seminars and symposia to debate the position of women in their societies. They conducted training workshops to increase women's self-confidence, raise their awareness and to expose them to new technical and management skills. They began to look more seriously at women's economic role, their contribution to and their position in their society, and they began to organize and plan projects that seriously attempted to address the needs of women at the community level. Some of these groups also began to press for legislation that would benefit women by removing all forms of discrimination and providing better services and more opportunities for women in all spheres.

These activities to a large extent provided an outlet for the creative energy and a medium through which the voices of ordinary women in every territory could be heard. They have helped to engender among women new awareness of their own strength, potential and sense of worth and have given them a vision of the possibility of achieving personal and national goals by means of cooperation, shared responsibility and the creative use of the collective capabilities of the entire population.

The work of the NGOs and the influence of regional and international initiatives has led Caribbean governments to increase their efforts to address women's issues in their countries. During the 1970s some countries set up advisory committees or national commissions on the status of women (Jamaica 1972, Barbados, Grenada and Trinidad 1976) and national governmental machinery has followed gradually.

National Machinery

During the last decade national machinery has been established in nine territories in the region. This machinery is seen as the focal point for women's issues and is responsible for working to improve the social, economic, political and legal status of women. It is intended to be a catalyst through which women and women's organizations can not only call for this improvement but can monitor and assess governmental policies. The functioning of this machinery has been erratic and has varied from territory to territory. In many cases their function has not been clearly defined; they face problems of the inadequate provision of financial and human resources; they have been shifted from one ministry to another. Many have become involved in running special programmes for women and have not been seen as an integral part of national development planning. In spite of this, and in the face of serious constraints such as lack of clear guidelines, a staff of one to three persons has usually attempted to respond in small ways to the needs of women in the various territories.

Legal Reforms

During the last decade there have been significant legal reforms in various territories to eliminate discrimination against women. Much of this has been in the area of family law. Family courts have been established in some countries and maternity law and equal pay for equal work laws have been introduced. Serious attempts have also been made by various groups to educate women about the law and to increase their awareness of their rights and privileges by seminars, printed material and through the print and electronic media.

Caribbean Celebration 1985

In March 1985 three hundred Caribbean women from all walks of life in the English- French- and Dutch-speaking territories met for three days to celebrate the achievements of Caribbean women during the UN Decade. They evaluated the wide range of initiatives and activities that had taken place. They critically analysed the strategies that had been adopted and the issues that had been addressed. They identified new areas of concern, such as the increase in sexual violence against women and the growing social tensions in the region, and committed themselves to address these with new vigour during the next decade. They also called on the governments of the region to reassess their present development strategies and do more than pay lip-service to women's problems in the region. They urged regional governments to accept that the full and equal participation of women in the development of the region could lead the way towards new development alternatives.

The celebration brought together women of all classes and ethnic groups—urban and rural women, educated, professional women and women farmers, lawyers, doctors, teachers, painters, poets, housewives, unemployed women, youth, single, married and divorced women—and united them in a common purpose. This was a true indication of the collective strength, solidarity and power of the Caribbean women's movement. Social attitudes are the greatest barrier to women's participation to national development; but before any attempts to bring about changes in these can be effective and meaningful, change must take place first on a personal level. It is through self-development that Caribbean women are making their contribution to the social, economic and political life of the region. It is through collective action and the judicious use of their latent power that they can help to bring about the necessary change in the social attitudes that are obstacles to their full equality as partners in the development of the region.

Women and Development in the Caribbean

Caribbean Women have always been integrally involved in the social and economic development of their societies; but their contribution to the development of the region has not been fully appreciated by planners and policy-makers. In the post-independence decades of the 1960s and 1970s, as Caribbean governments searched for ways to maintain their small independent nations, they adopted development models based on the concept of economic growth. There was rapid expansion of a manufacturing and industrial sector and a shift to production for export which with hindsight did not stimulate the economy to the degree that had been expected and which has in fact resulted in greater dependence on foreign capital.

During this period too many governments implemented large-scale development projects in the rural areas. These projects, mostly funded by external aid, were conceived by economic planners without any input from the rural population—the women and men who were to be involved and who were expected to benefit from the projects. No attempts were made to pay attention to the special contribution that women could have made to these projects or to the likely impact of the projects on the lives of rural women. Most of these projects were large, expensive and unwieldy and tended to focus on the provision of infrastructure and physical resources.

Neither of these strategies—expansion of the industrial sector or the implementation of large-scale development projects—has had many positive effects on the lives of women in the region. In the first case, although quite a significant number of women have found jobs in this sector, the way has been opened for women to be more widely exploited as cheap, unskilled labour. In the second case, because women's economic role in agricultural production continued to remain invisible, the only aspect that was seen to be relevant to women was often an appended 'home economics component'.

The failure of these growth oriented models in the Caribbean, and elsewhere in the developing world, has led in the decade of the 1980s to the emergence of a concept of bottom-up participatory development in which the emphasis is on people. This recognition of the need for a more people-centred approach is gradually forcing governments and development planners to pay attention to the development of human resources. In this context it is critical that they recognize the role of women. Governments now accept that development must be defined more broadly and must involve the more equitable distribution of resources, the reduction of poverty and unemployment, the improvement of the quality of life for the majority of the population and the removal of existing inequalities, including sexual inequalities. These issues have now become central to the rhetoric and plans for national development.

Women in Development

The concept of Women in Development (WID) which emerged out of International Women's Year helped to focus governments' attention on the important roles that women play and the valuable contributions that they make to the development of their societies. This in turn created a need for planners to find out more about women and to hear women's views on the development process. In order to meet this need for information on and about women a great deal of research has been undertaken in the Caribbean—as elsewhere. The research has revealed that women perceive, encounter and experience the development process in ways that are significantly different from men. Women have begun to articulate more forcibly their opinions on development issues and are expressing the view that development should result in the provision of basic needs for all families, a more equal distribution and sharing of resources, an improvement in the quality of life for the poor and the disadvantaged in society and in the peaceful coexistence of all peoples. Theirs is a vision of the world that focuses on the factor hitherto missing in earlier development theories—the human factor.

The goal of integrating women fully into the development process can neither be seen in global terms nor achieved by an agenda fixed by global parameters, nor can it be legislated for. Its achievement is possible only through strategies developed within a specific cultural and social context. Within the Caribbean, therefore, the UN Decade for Women must be seen within the context of the struggle of Caribbean people for individual and collective self-reliance and autonomy. Since 1977 a variety of strategies, programmes and projects focused on the role of women in Caribbean development, have been implemented with some positive results. The lessons learnt and the insights gained are valuable and have helped to ensure that some of women's concerns are being taken into consideration in national development planning.

Strategies

One important strategy has been the use of research to sensitize and inform planners and policy-makers on the situation of women and the problems that they face. Prior to 1975 very little research had been done on the lives of Caribbean women; that which had been carried out had tended to focus on their reproductive rather than on their productive roles. Social research findings from censuses and social and household surveys did not in most cases include much data that was broken down by sex. The data base on Caribbean women was therefore very scanty. By 1980, with more attention being paid to women's concerns and with the recognition that these should be addressed within the context of national planning, the need for specific information on all aspects of women's lives had become apparent. It has also been realized that it is important that research on women's lives provides insight on how women perceive their own social reality as against how men—male planners and researchers—perceive it. This has led to a significant increase in the number of women researchers doing research on women as well as in the amount of research that is being done. More emphasis is now being placed on qualitative data and on the use of more interactive participatory methods. A variety of research activities on women have taken place in the Caribbean over the last five years. These have ranged from the large (macro) regional Women in the Caribbean Project to small (micro) community level studies.

Macro-research Projects—The Women in the Caribbean Project: This three-year research project was coordinated and conducted by the Institute of Social and Economic Research (ISER) UWI Cave Hill between 1980 and 1982. Within this project a multi-level method was used. It included a sample survey of 1,526 women from Antigua, Barbados and St Vincent, in-depth interviews with a small sub-sample of 39 women, and a series of investigations in six other countries to provide data on different sectors such as women in public life, rural women, women in education and attitudes held by women and by men about women.

It used a team of women researchers, involved community workers in the research process and collected and analysed the data in relation to three main themes: sources of livelihood, emotional support and power and authority. The results of this research were presented at an international conference held in Barbados in 1982 and a number of monographs have been published by the ISER. These include the following titles: *Women and the Family, Women in Politics, Women and the Law, Perceptions of Women* and *Women and Education.*

The Economic Role of Women in Small-scale Agriculture in the Eastern Caribbean—St Lucia: This survey was conducted in 1981 as part of the Caribbean Agricultural Extension Project. The five-year project (CAEP) was jointly sponsored by the UWI Faculty of Agriculture and the Mid-Western Universities Consortium of International Aid (MUCIA). Its main objective was to upgrade existing extension services and to provide more adequate services to small farmers throughout the region. The survey was carried out by WAND, UWI, Women in Development (WID) Barbados, and the MUCIA-WID group and the Caribbean Research Centre (CRC), St Lucia.

The questionnaires were administered to adults in 290 farm households and interviews were conducted with 195 women within these households. A unique feature of this research project is that the data was not interpreted by the two researchers—consultants from MUCIA-WID but at a regional workshop held for this purpose in St Lucia. Participants at this workshop included government officials, agriculture extension officers, the interviewers—all local St Lucians, representatives from regional agencies involved in agriculture, from UWI, from Caricom, from CAEP and from MUCIA. This strategy allowed a wide cross-section of key persons in the region to directly infuence and be influenced by the results of the survey and increased the possibility of the data being used to influence policy on agricultural development. Some of the recommendations which emerged out of the survey have been implemented both at regional level within CAEP and at national level in the national plan for agricultural development in St Lucia. In the case of the latter one direct result has been the imnplementation of an integrated Rural Development Project in three communities in St Lucia.

The Impact of Large-scale Development Schemes on Rural Households and on Women: The research project was sponsored by WAND and the Population Council of NY and was carried out in 1982-83 in Jamaica, Dominica and St Lucia in collaboration with the respective governments. In each case a well established large-scale rural development scheme was chosen and an attempt made to assess its impact on the women and rural households in the communities in which it had been implemented. In each country the research was conducted by a team comprising a social scientist researcher, an official from the national planning agency, a representative from the Ministry of Agriculture or the Ministry of Community Development and a representative of the national machinery for women (women's desk). A second tier team comprised persons from a wide cross-section of the society who had had links with the project—representatives of marketing boards, cooperatives and project directors. This team provided support and critical advice to the research team.

Before the research began researchers held lengthy discussions with community members in each target community, with those who had been originally involved in conceptualization and implementation of the project and with government officials. During the field-work phase questionnaires were administered, interviews conducted and community meetings and discussions were organized and recorded. Research teams from the three countries met periodically to discuss and develop common approaches as the basis for comparative analysis. At national workshops held in each country a wide cross-section of community people and government officials analysed and interpreted the data and at the end of the project the results were presented in a regional workshop by government representatives and officials. The most significant outcome of this research project was the sensitization of planners and policy-makers to the fact that the impact of large-scale development projects can be minimal or even negative if the concerns and needs of women and of rural households are not incorporated at the planning stages. A casebook of the findings has been published and includes guidelines to planners.

Micro-community Studies: A number of small-scale research studies have also been carried out. These have produced data on women's social reality and have provided a vehicle through which women themselves, at the community level, can analyse and critically reflect on their position within the larger social system. In many of these studies the participatory research approach has been used and the research process has been a vehicle for education and skills training as well as a tool for collective social action.

Women in rural communities in St Vincent, St Lucia and Grenada have, with the help of professional women researchers and on their own, developed research instruments to collect detailed information on their communities, their lives and themselves. They have conducted surveys, administered questionnaires, conducted individual and group interviews, taped life stories and done archival work. They have developed community profiles and case-studies. They have used many innovative techniques—role plays, community drama, poetry and drawings—to record and share the results of their research with the entire community. They have interpreted and analysed the data they have collected and have used it to build programmes and projects in an attempt to find solutions to some of their pressing problems. This approach has demystified the research process and moved it from being the exclusive preserve of the expert researcher to being a tool in the hands of ordinary people. The results of some of these micro-studies have been shared at national and regional levels and have been used to supplement the findings of macro-research projects.

The Caribbean Association for Feminist Research and Action (CAFRA)
The amount of research that needs to be done on Caribbean women has resulted in a significant increase in the number of women researchers. At the same time, there is a growing recognition in the region that unless research on women is done by researchers who are *sensitive* to women's issues and concerns, the data which is obtained is very likely to be distorted or misinterpreted. It is also realized that research activity on women in the region is in its infancy and that there are large areas of women's lives and experiences about which very little is known.

The Caribbean Association of Feminist Research and Action (CAFRA), a newly formed organization, is attempting to address some of these issues. Formed in 1984 it was formally launched in March 1985 at the Caribbean Celebration. Its objectives are to build linkages between and provide support to women who are involved in research and action programmes, and to sensitize and bring a feminist perspective to women researchers.

Projects and Programmes for Women in Development
Another strategy that has been widely used in an attempt to facilitate greater participation of women in the development process is the implementation of a number of women's projects. Over the last ten years there has been a dramatic increase in the number of small projects for women. Many of these were inspired by international rhetoric and have been supported by funds from international agencies. On the whole they have failed to bring women into the mainstream of material development, but rather have effectively kept them on the periphery.

The reasons for failure have been many. Some of these projects were intended to help women to generate income; but the participants in these projects did not have the necessary skills or had not been involved in planning the project and when the initial, short-term funding ran out the project collapsed. Most of these projects had been conceived, planned and implemented without any attempts to link or relate them to national economic goals or priorities.

At the same time a number of women were being exposed to training in leadership skills through their participation in short, ad hoc one day and weekend workshops. Again the effect was minimal as the objectives of such programmes had not been clearly thought through. The training did not seem to lead women anywhere and since there was usually no follow up it has been very difficult to assess its impact. In most cases the majority of these small projects were not based on any research about women's needs and priorities so that the women themselves soon lost interest.

During the last five years the lessons learnt from these failures have resulted in a more serious attempt to develop programmes and projects that have more realistic objectives, that are based on an examination and analysis of women's needs and that attempt to provide a framework within which women's needs can be understood and met within the wider societal context and in relation to national development goals.

These new attempts have by and large been of a more integrated nature and have some or all of the following components built in: consciousness-raising and awareness-building (for participants and project planners), research-needs assessment and problem solving, a basic adult non-formal education or literacy programme, training in a variety of skills (technical and managerial), ongoing participatory planning and evaluation and income-earning. Using this integrated package a small number of projects throughout the region have been very successful.

A woodworking project for young mothers to produce nursery school furniture in Grenada, an education project with market women and a skills training programme in welding for unemployed women in Jamaica, an appropriate technology and garment making project in Guyana all had these components built into them and all achieved some measure of success. These have pointed the way for more such projects to be implemented in a number of rural communities.

A pilot project for the integration of Women in Rural Development implemented in St Vincent in 1980 using this approach has had tremendous success and is still going well. A similar larger integrated rural development project implemented in three rural communities in St Lucia is also proving to be beneficial for the women and communities involved. In both of these projects a ripple effect has been achieved in the entire community by involving women and government officials from the initial stages in the planning. The experiences and successful outcomes of these projects have been documented and shared with other women, with NGOs and with government officials, planners and policy-makers at the regional and national levels. Already in small ways the results have begun to influence development projects that will address women's needs and involve them more meaningfully in national development.

Part 1: Women and History

Chapter 1: Nanny

Nanny was a leader of the Maroons at the beginning of the 18th Century. She was known by both the Maroons and the British settlers as an outstanding military leader who became, in her lifetime and after, a symbol of unity and strength for her people during times of crisis. She was particularly important to them in the fierce fight with the British during the First Maroon War from 1720-39. Although she has been immortalized in songs and legends, certain facts about Nanny (or 'Granny Nanny', as she was affectionately known) have also been documented. A nanny was also a type of chieftainess or wise woman of the village who passed down legends and who encouraged the continuation of customs, music and songs that had come with the people from Africa, and who instilled in them confidence and pride.

All legends and documents refer to Nanny of the First Maroon War as the most outstanding women of this time, leading her people with courage and inspiring them to maintain that spirit of freedom, that life of independence which was their rightful inheritance.

Chapter 2: Some Factors Affecting Women in the Caribbean Past and Present

by Rhoda Reddock

At the beginning of the 1980s a new mood informs women still committed to the total emancipation of women and of all humanity. There is a need for an international women's movement which transcends but understands the existing divisions. From the experience of the developmentalist approach we can learn the importance of planning, organization and structure; from the radical feminists we can learn the importance of autonomy over our lives and in our organizations; while from the socialist feminists we can learn to analyse our reality from an historical and materialist perspective in order to better comprehend the forces which determine our existence; from the ordinary women who have not been part of these activities we can learn the art of struggling daily and consistently to achieve our aims.

From very early in Caribbean history, the control of women has been a crucial element in maintaining the power of the oppressor groups. Carib Indians raided Arawak settlements and captured the women to make use of their skills as agriculturalists. The strict sexual division of labour in Carib settlements was reinforced by language differences between men and women; men spoke one language, and women another.

During slavery the use of women as concubines by white men helped to create social divisions based on colour. The male bias in Caribbean history interpreted the sexual relationships between white colonists and slave women as instances of woman's treacherous collusion with oppressors rather than as part of a complex system of sex-gender relations of the oppressive slave society and economy. A closer look at Caribbean society and history could reveal a great deal about the intricate relationship between sex, class and race as forms of oppression.

In the Caribbean, African women slaves worked alongside men in the field. There was little sexual division of labour. There is evidence that during the period of slavery, women resisted having children and did not regard motherhood as an instinctive or automatically natural role. These two important aspects of women's history in the Caribbean raise questions about much of what is considered to be natural to women throughout the world and could be a focus of further research.

After the abolition of the slave-trade, and ultimately of slavery, Western European forms of household organization began to be adopted. With the advent of wage-labour some system for the reproduction of labour power had to be instituted. It was after the abolition of the slave-trade that the ideology of Western marriage was actively encouraged and a greater sexual division of labour encouraged. Men began to be paid more than women in spite of the experience during slavery of women performing better under hard conditions. Fewer jobs were available for women. Women began to work less regularly in order to combine work with household production and the raising of their own children. On small plots of land women developed networks of skill-sharing, child-caring and child sharing. It has yet to be ascertained whether these traditions reinforced women's subordination or acted as institutions of resistance.

These networks, which appear on the surface to alleviate the burdens of discrimination based on gender, must also be seen in the context of the wider society. The reality there was, and still is, that peasant producers own the worst land. The land barons control all the largest and best acreage. The entire peasant population of Jamaica, for example, was to a greater or lesser extent dependent on this system. The position of strength of women within the sphere of domestic production, therefore, is counterbalanced by the weakness of the peasant economy and the need for cash.

With the advent of the 'development decades', capital began to pull male labour not simply to nearby plantations but to wherever employment in industry was needed. This tendency to offer more wage work to men rather than to women has meant that today in Jamaica 40% fewer women are involved in social production than during the immediate post-emancipation period. This means that women work more in the hidden sectors of the economy—as unpaid food producers and processors, housewives and petty traders. Many women are therefore dependent on, but at the same time marginalized by, underdeveloped capitalism.

The weak position of women on the labour market is both derived from, and results in, women's dependence on the male wage and the concept of the male breadwinner. This reinforces women's subordinate position in the household. In exchange for cash, women give their labour and sexual services. The fact that the male wage is itself often irregular means that relationships frequently break down. Outside the household women who do wage work do domestic-related tasks, which, like those in the home, are low paid and carry low status. Recent indications are that the situation of women in the Caribbean is getting worse. In Jamaica, for example, approximately 40% of women are unemployed as against 16% of men. Of employed women, 68% are doing unskilled labour and earning less than J$30 per week. At the same time, one-third of the women are de facto heads of households.

In the Caribbean, because of its unique history as a relatively new cosmopolitan region recently emerging from direct colonial rule, the general problems of women internationally assume a new dimension. Questions specific to our history and societies have yet to be answered. The failure to examine the experience of 51% of the Caribbean population in earlier research and analyses calls into severe question the validity of those findings, as well as the suitability of the solutions derived to the Caribbean

Part 2: Women and Labour

Chapter 3: Employment of Women Workers in the Caribbean

by Peggy Antrobus

There has always been a significant percentage of women in employment in the Caribbean. Under slavery, women worked side by side with men in the fields. In fact, in the later period of slavery women outnumbered male workers on the plantations.

From those early days, however, they were subjected to discrimination as they were denied the opportunities for training which were available to a select few of the men and so were excluded from the factories and the supervisory positions which were later open to the men.

According to figures published by the International Labour Organization (ILO), Caribbean countries are among those having high female activity rates (that is, participation in the labour force). Over 20% of the female population in the Caribbean is economically active—comparing favourably with the world average of about 28%. This figure is almost twice as high as the figure for Latin America, the region into which the Caribbean is often absorbed in international categorization. In the age range 25-44, the female activity rate for the Caribbean is actually higher than the world figure of 48%. In Jamaica for example, 62% of the female population over fourteen years of age is in the labour force. In Barbados nearly 40% of the labour force is female—and this is a good (slightly above) average for the CARICOM countries. These high female participation rates conceal facts which demonstrate the unequal status of women in employment in the countries of the region:

1. About 70% of the women in employment are in low paid, low skilled, marginal jobs in domestic and other services.
2. The majority of women in employment are in 'traditonal' occupations such as services, teaching, nursing, secretarial etc.—in other words performing stereotyped jobs.
3. Only a very small percentage of the jobs in administration and management are held by women (12% in Jamaica, probably among the highest in the region)—and this despite the fact that the educational performance of girls up to secondary level is at least equal to that of the boys while at university level female enrolment is nearly as high as male.
4. Unemployment among women in the labour force is everywhere higher than it is among men—in Jamaica and Barbados it is twice as high; according to the *Report of the Barbados Commission on the Status of*

Women in December 1977, 64.4% of the unemployed were women. In Jamaica in 1975, 32% of the female labour force was unemployed compared to 12% of the male labour force—figures for the other CARICOM countries would probably reflect a similar situation.

However, these figures present only a partial view of the true situation of women in employment in the Caribbean. We must also recognize from the outset that:

(a) Lack of opportunities for employment in rural areas affects women more adversely than men, as evidenced both by the higher unemployment figures among women (in some rural parishes in Jamaica the unemployment among women is four times as high as it is among men) as well as by the fact (in Jamaica at any rate) that the majority of emigrants from rural to urban areas are women.

(b) A smaller percentage of women workers are unionized than men—because of their concentration in services and informal sector activities.

We should of course recognize that 'there is no officially declared policy for the suppression of women educationally, socially, industrially, legally or economically in the Caribbean'. Quite the contrary: official policy, even of the most discriminatory type, is usually couched in terms which show a 'concern' for the welfare of women and even a recognition of the importance of their contribution to society. Again, to use prejudice and discrimination against women is 'seldom with deliberate or malicious intent'. Existing practices are, in fact, the result of deeply ingrained attitudes of which the holders are often unconscious. These attitudes and beliefs have acquired the authority of 'natural laws', are internalized and accepted by many women themselves and are unlikely to change in the foreseeable futgure—either in the Caribbean or elsewhere.

Chapter 4: Women in Caribbean Agriculture

by Lorna Gordon

At various times, women have been referred to as 'the salt of the earth', 'the poorest of the poor', 'the backbone of the economy'. They toil to feed and sustain society, yet their contribution to agriculture's share of the Gross Domestic Product and Gross National Product is rarely reflected in the statistical indices of economic growth.

While much has been learnt about the nature of women's work and their multiple roles in recent years, there is still tremendous ignorance of the social, economic and political factors governing the survival, behaviour, relationships, priorities and aspirations of rural women in agriculture. Research into the totality of their lives has either been ignored or neglected because of the low status accorded the peasant class, class-biased notions and presumptions about their existence, the scarcity of women researchers to record their experiences and views and the protective invisibility of rural women themselves. Perhaps the greatest lack has been the words of rural women expressing their views, articulating their feelings and defining their priorities.

Since the mid-1970s, there has been a growing consciousness, supported by vital data, that these hardworking, shrewd and productive women are agents, not simply beneficiaries of development. That they are not merely welfare problems but resources upon which development planners should draw. This awareness complements the broader vision reflected in the goals of the United Nations Second Development Decade and the United Nations Decade for Women, which equate rural development with a far-reaching transformation of the social and economic structures, the institutions, relationships and processes which shape the quality of rural life.

In the Caribbean, where underdevelopment emanates directly from the particular social and institutional character of the plantation system of resource organization, initiatives to change that structure must underpin the efforts of women seeking integration into the developmental process. Without this, it is clear that women, who comprise some 50% of the Caribbean rural population, will continue to be disadvantaged and discriminated against in various ways by:

(a) customs, institutions and attitudes which will continue to marginalize women's economic inputs;

(b) statistical indices of economic growth which will fail to record women's

work, time and multiple roles;
(c) the weakness of inter-sectoral linkages which will deny women the services to meet their particular needs and access to benefits from development;
(d) public policies which will continue to deny rural areas a fair share of public investment, to the detriment of women;
(e) pricing policies, taxation and terms of trade which will continue to favour the urban-industrial sector, depressing rural income and negating women's productive skills;
(f) sexism which will continue to undermine women's effective participation and involvement in decision-making and benefit-sharing.

Most rural areas in the Caribbean fall between two extremes. They are either villages on the periphery of modern urban progress or villages poorly endowed with natural resources and largely isolated from the larger economy.

In the face of urbanization—attracting more men to industrial wage-labour—and continuing migration, women in agriculture are feeling the full effects of the historical conflict between the needs of the planter class and those of the peasant smallholder class. The needs and values of the export-oriented, urban plantation economy have only aggravated the plight of women in the subsistence-oriented, rural agricultural economy.

In 1981, four agencies collaborated in *A Survey of the Economic Role of Women in Small-scale Agriculture in St Lucia*. The project was set within the context of a larger regional project for the improvement of Agricultural Extension Services in the Eastern Caribbean. While the research involved a relatively small sample (245 farm households, comprising 1,415 persons), the findings address the relative situation of all women in agriculture in the English-speaking Caribbean; they are all faced with the same structural, institutional and technological problems. The findings further corroborate those of a 1981 *Study of the Situation of Rural Families and Rural Women in Agriculture, Forestry and Fishing* undertaken in three selected areas in rural Jamaica. Both reports, and the data supplied by various other sources, paint a dismal picture of the objective conditions of women in agriculture and, by extension, women in the rural economy.

The Nature of Women's Work in the Agricultural Sectors

Women play a major economic role in agriculture in the Caribbean as farm workers, farmers, farm labourers, heads of farm households and marketers of agricultural produce. They account for 30% of the agricultural labour force in St Vincent, 47% in St Lucia and over 50% in Montserrat and Antigua. Between 30 and 50% of female heads of households are engaged in agriculture and such related activities as forestry, fishing and agro-industry. Women are primarily self-employed subsistence farmers, landless labourers and producers/traders. They almost completely dominate the distribution and retailing of locally grown food crops. Since the 1930s they have shifted from mainly provision production to a mixed provision and export crop production, cultivating sugar, bananas, citrus, coconuts and a variety of vegetables.

Their working day starts between 5 and 6 a.m. They prepare breakfast for the family and attend to the young (nursing, bathing, preparing for school) before heading to the fields. In five to six hours of work, they might engage in weeding, hoeing, planting, reaping and food storage. About two hours are devoted to domestic animal husbandry (taking livestock to pasture or for water, milking the cows, collecting eggs). Another three to four hours must be found for such household chores as cleaning, washing, ironing, collecting water, firewood, and supervising the processing and preparation of food for the family. This can involve grinding, husking, pounding of grains, drying, sifting and threshing.

For women in forestry, employed seasonally in mainly nursery work, their workday includes transporting soil for the setting of seeds, potting, weeding and culling dead or drying plants. Women in fisheries engage predominantly in marketing. Miscellaneous chores such as inventory-taking, accounting, sewing and personal family business occupy all these women into late evening. In any given week, their time may be further extended by external duties related to the family and community.

The producer/trader must find a day to sell some 70–80% of the food grown in the market-place. Some operate stalls for the sale of craft and consumer items, others prepare ready-cooked meals and beverages for sale in open restaurants. Invariably they have responsibility for the health of their families. There is also household shopping to be done. At the community level, midwifery, teaching and child care may be required, as well as cooperative efforts at house and road repairs, construction, food processing and food preservation.

Incomes and Employment Among Women in Agriculture

In the agricultural sector, farming is subsidized by wage labour. A sizable proportion of women receive some cash assistance from remittances sent by children and relatives residing overseas. Approximately 96% of all income is used for household purposes. A major part of the disposable income is spent on food. In a sector of economy where women comprise some 40% of the labour force, and where there is less evidence of the polarized division of labour characteristic of the modern industrial wage sector, differential wages are paid according to the sex of the workers.

In Jamaica, 34% of female agricultural workers earned between J$20-50 weekly in 1980. In the survey, 61 out of 100 respondents earned monthly incomes of J$77-200. The average daily wage paid to a female citrus worker in Trinidad, in 1976, was TT$4. For the male worker, the wage was TT$5.10. In copra, males earned TT$6.98, females $5.34. In St Lucia, the guaranteed minimum daily wage paid for general agricultural labour in 1982 was EC$9.36 for females, $10.41 for males. Vincentian female workers earned EC$10.00, men $13.00. In February 1982, at the height of a wage dispute in the Barbados sugar industry, the out-of-crop hourly wages payable to plantation, estate and factory workers proposed by the government were: men, A-Class, BDS$2.96, women, A-Class, BDS$2.45. In the B-Class, there was a 57¢ discrepancy in favour of men. Among general workers the offer was: males BDS$2.96 per hour, females BDS$2.45.

That the discrepancies were unaltered in the final negotiated settlement underlines the fact that women are not usually involved in trade union negotiations for workers' wages and working conditions. The unequal sharing of poverty between women and men in the Caribbean rural economy is further exacerbated by the competition against each other for scarce job opportunities to earn cash income. It is not uncommon to see groups of female and male general agricultural labourers moving from district to district, in response to shifting demands for labour.

The Distribution and Access to Productive Assets

Access to land and capital and their efficient use and preservation as resources represent power. A skewed pattern of land distribution has endowed former plantations with almost all the flat, fertile lands and the peasants with the hilly, shallow-soiled and relatively infertile lands. In the Eastern Caribbean, farms of 100 acres and above account for 42%, and 83% of total land acreage. In Barbados alone, 264 plantations hold 87.5% of total available land (64,186 acres) as against 12,629 small farms with 12.5% (9,131 acres) of mainly poor quality land. In Jamaica up to 1968, 21% of farms island-wide controlled 88% of available land, while 79% of farmers owning between 0-5 acres, controlled 12% of the land.

Thus in marked contrast to the peasant sector which survives on mainly one-plot (71% in St Lucia), family land (40%, St Lucia) averaging 4.4 acres and less, and purchased plots owned by 30% of all small farmers, the plantation sector is well endowed with the best farm lands, modern technology, credit facilities and organized markets. To the extent that this is the dominant pattern of land distribution, and to the extent that Caribbean women in agriculture have rights, they have little or no control over acquiring either the volume or quality of arable land which could affect the degree, mode and quality of their production.

Despite various attempts at land resettlement, cooperative farming and other forms of land redistribution, the essential character of land ownership has remained unchanged. It is clear that the resource endowment and capacity for development among women in Caribbean agriculture are not commensurate with their numerical importance in the sector. Access to financial capital is a further critical problem.

In the book-keeping system of development, female farming is not viewed by commercial financial institutions as suitable or viable for venture capital investment. The absence of female farmers from the policy-making bodies of crop lien schemes,* revolving loan funds, cooperative credit unions and banks, commodity boards, and self-supporting farmers' loan schemes impedes their access to fixed and developmental capital. In the allocation and delivery of technology, agricultural information, equipment, tools and transport facilities, there is a male-sexist bias which obscures women's needs. Access to the rental and hire of farm machines, planting implements and tools is minimal and costly. As a consequence of their inability to secure legitimate resources to develop and maintain economic viability, and to acquire labour-efficient and cost-reducing technology, rural women, in frustration, are becoming increasingly alienated from the land.

Provision of Infrastructure to Help Women

In almost all survey data, the majority of women in agriculture cite the need for land, finances, roads and transport, housing, electricity, water supplies as primary basic needs. With the possible exception of banana boxing plants, crop collection facilities are widely scattered. Women may spend many hours journeying on foot, sometimes covering 10 or more miles. Market outlets, shopping complexes and medical facilities are often sited in towns and cities at considerable distances from the farm location and very few rural women own private transport. Where transportation has to be hired, it is costly and not always reliable. Limited supplies of piped water, electricity, cooking gas and even kerosene force nearly two-thirds of rural women to live without such modern conveniences as flush toilet facilities, refrigerators, electric irons, floor polishers, gas stoves and telephones. The collection of wood and charcoal for fuel continues—an arduous, time-consuming daily task. Despite the visibility of a high percentage of pre-school- and school-age children, women in agricultural areas have virtually no access to day-care centres and library or recreational facilities.

The Quality of Education among Women in Agriculture

Inadequate general education and lack of specialized education continue to reduce women's ability to make cost-reducing improvements (technologically and organizationally) in their farming practices, or to diversify into other occupations to broaden the economic base of their communities. The overwhelming majority of women in both the St Lucia and Jamaica survey have either never been to school, or have had only primary education. Most (another 79.5%) have never had specialized agricultural training. Almost all

---

*Schemes in which farmers are permitted to borrow a certain amount of cash against their projected crop/produce.

the women acquired their farming knowledge from their parents or circle of acquaintances. The enrolment of female agriculture students in special institutions is still relatively low.

By the 1980s the UWI's Faculty of Agriculture had admitted 148 females to 190 males. In 1977-8 there were 18 females on the degree course, compared to 39 males. At the former Jamaica School of Agriculture, in 1979, females accounted for 164 enrolments (or 31.1%), males 363 (or 68%). Trade and vocational centres have been mainly designed for male workers, garment schools being the possible exception. Many rural women consequently continue to be trained for cottage industry employment and become maids or domestic servants for the local urban and overseas markets. There is still a critical need for a range of farm-related skills associated with using and dispensing credit, operating and managing agro-industrial enterprises, produce stores, repair businesses and vocational skills such as equipment repair and maintenance, electrical installation and building construction.

It is obvious from the available data that the life of women in Caribbean agriculture is severely limited by a range of forces operating in their social, economic and political environment. Their human development will necessitate radical departures from existing policies and initiatives to deal with the structure of power relationships which contribute to their underdevelopment.

Very few can spare the time from economic and domestic activities for active membership of groups outside their social network or church. Yet, by membership in policy-making economic, social and political institutions, by regular attendance, participation, voting on issues, and holding official posts, they can bring their influence to bear. Enlightened self-confidence will encourage women on the farms to increase their decision-making power (in more than 40% of cases, men make decisions alone) over major issues concerning the management of the farm and production. In short, chance has never yet satisfied the hope of a suffering people. Only action, self-reliance and a wider vision of self and future can help women in Caribbean agriculture to enjoy the light of their own freedom.

Chapter 5: Domestic Workers

by Patricia Mohammed

It is painfully clear in many ways that a negative value is placed on housework and household workers in the Caribbean. The Industrial Relations Act (1972) of Trinidad and Tobago decrees that "household workers" are *not* workers under law. As such, they do not come under the protection of labour laws designed to look after the interests of workers in that country. In all the territories of the Caribbean, the Gross National Product and National Income accounts do not include the value of household work and related activities.

There are numerous difficulties in trying to impute a monetary or social value to housework and to household workers' efforts; but it is apparent that housework, whether carried out for pay or in an unpaid situation, is viewed as "non-work". It is assigned a negative, and often demeaning, status in the hierarchy of work roles. The domestic worker, therefore, automatically fills a low status position in society as determined by the definitions of social class which rely on occupational classification. Of even greater concern is the fact that domestic labour includes some of the most repetitive, tedious, unfulfilling and rewarding tasks; that it is normally carried out in isolation from other workers; and that women comprise the large majority of domestic workers. These workers are among the most exploited on the labour market today.

But before we examine the conditions under which domestic workers function in the Caribbean, let us first understand why housework attracts such negative attitudes in society and why women predominate as workers in this category. Housework has a low status value attached to it for several reasons. Most of us are mindful that domestic labour is basic to society and involves the reproduction of daily life itself. The housewife's day is made up of the early morning chaos of rushed breakfast, unmade beds, unswept floors, mountains of wash, trips to the shop and market perhaps accompanied by the unceasing demands of young children. Housework is monotonous, mindless and uninspiring. At the end of it all the meals are eaten, the house becomes untidy again, the clothes soiled and no evidence remains to show the effort which has been expended.

"Work", as we know, has come to be associated with labour outside the home, done for a wage or salary, where the mental or manual labour which has gone into it remains concretely evident. Under the present economic system in the English-speaking Caribbean, skill-training and education are highly valued and rewards are naturally greater in those areas where skilled or trained labour is in low supply; therefore housework, which requires little formal training, is given a very low rating. In addition, the highly distorted value system of our post-colonial societies continues to place white-collar occupations and interests above other, similarly vital labouring occupations.

Why are domestic workers mainly women? Housework has historically been assigned to women as their domain of work, a domain which has come to be accepted in many cultures throughout the world. This relegation of household tasks to women evolved out of the interplay between women's biological make-up—their capacity to reproduce the society and thus the labour force—and the demands of the economy to produce surplus goods and services for the survival and reproduction of the society. Housework is not, as is popularly believed, the "natural" domain of women. Traditionally, this cultural assignment has withstood many generations and women are prepared from early childhood, through the socialization process within the family, for the roles of housekeeping and child-rearing. Within the formal education system this tradition continues, for implicit in women's training is the view that they are to make good mothers, wives and housekeepers while men are geared for the role of breadwinner in the family.

In the history of Caribbean society, the majority of women have carried the double role of economically supporting their families, as well as performing the daily household chores. With the shift from agriculture to industrialization, women who formerly worked as unskilled labourers in agriculture were forced into the labour market, many of them unprepared for the kinds of skills now demanded of them. Many women were thus forced to seek employment in the only area in which they were "trained"—domestic service. With the expansion of the education system, the state and private sector, more job opportunities have become available to women; but they are faced with a continuing battle to compete for jobs with the male labour force in areas which are still deemed "masculine".

In the more developed and larger economies of the Caribbean, such as Trinidad and Tobago and Jamaica, more jobs outside the home have become available for women. More employed women in these countries thus require domestic help. As a result, there is greater demand for domestic help among the upper and middle classes in these societies. The availability of jobs, as well as the dire need for employment, shifts women from rural to urban communities, from the smaller to the larger Caribbean islands and from the Caribbean itself to such countries as the United States and Canada. This shift of labour involves many young women between the ages of 18-25. Their need to find a job, as well as to retain one when it is found, in some instances places these women in a very vulnerable position where they work under very unfair and possibly highly exploitative conditions. A surplus of unskilled workers makes for a greater supply than demand and thus for an easily expendable labour force. This partly explains why domestic workers face low wages and oppressive conditions.

A study carried out by the Housewives Association of Trinidad and Tobago

(HATT) in 1975 yields some vital and formerly undocumented information on the conditions under which domestic workers are employed. This study was carried out in Trinidad but the similarities observed between the islands make the findings relevant to the situation of domestic workers in other Caribbean territories. The HATT study was carried out in two phases; the first was a preliminary research study into the conditions of domestic workers, the second a sample survey of selected household workers and of selected households in the country. The study identified four types of household workers: sleep-in or live-in workers, whole-day workers, half-day workers and part-time workers. The duties performed by these workers ranged from general housework such as cleaning, washing and so on, to specialized services such as child-care and ironing. Some workers questioned in the survey were found to be working very long hours. Over 40% worked more than eight hours per day; sleep-in workers tended to work the longest hours, sometimes more than twelve hours a day, as volunteered by 25% of the respondents. Of the workers in the survey, 32% worked six-and-a-half to seven days a week, and a further 29% worked five-and-a-half to six days a week.

According to the conditions under which they are employed, domestic workers are given no protection against sickness, maternity and old age disabilities. The low wages for which they work make it impossible for them to make adequate provision for such needs on their own. In 1975, at the time of the HATT survey, the average weekly wage for household workers was TT$15.00. At that time also there was no legally stipulated or informally accepted minimum wage for domestic workers. Wages and other conditions of work were determined in a private agreement between employer and employee and benefits to the worker, if any, depended on the generosity of the individual employer. One of the strong recommendations at the conclusion of the study was the

> need for minimum wages and conditions of work to be fixed, to be accepted and used by the community on a voluntary basis in the first instance, but eventually as part of the legislation providing for minimum wages and conditions of service for all workers.

Several other important findings emerged from this study. Domestic workers complained of inadequate living and sleeping accommodation provided by their employers; of improper and discourteous modes of address from their employers and employers' offspring; and in some cases there were stringent restrictions on the visitors they were permitted to receive. On the other hand, employers complained of dissatisfaction with the kinds of services provided by domestic workers and the abuse of privileges extended to them. An interesting picture emerges of the entire domestic employee/employer relationship in the society. Despite the obvious and growing dependency of working and professional women on the services provided by domestic workers, and obversely on the need for many women to find employment as domestic workers, there exists a strong element of distrust between employer and employee, rooted in the class differences between these women. This is especially curious in the light of the particular work situation of the domestic employee which involves a certain level of intimacy and trust between employer and employee.

A spate of letters to the media in Trinidad and Tobago in response to the proposal by the newly appointed Minimum Wages Board, that minimum wages for domestic workers be set at TT$45.00 weekly, clearly indicated the sentiments of either side. The *Trinidad Guardian* 16 May 1979, carried a letter from one disgruntled female employer who suggested that domestic workers were already overpaid and over-indulged. She described domestic workers as "sly, lazy and overpaid", condemned their (alleged) theft of costly items from their employers and commented on the quantity and cost of meals eaten by domestics at their work-place. A reply to this kind of censure, as well as to the proposal of the Minimum Wages Board, was published in the same newspaper on 25 June 1979, and captioned "A Maid's Eye View". It was a long letter by a domestic worker who felt that the wages proposed by the Board were already below those received by domestics and were highly unrealistic in view of existing living conditions. She was very scathing of the treatment meted out to domestic workers by their employers and of the practice of some members of the society of hiring domestics purely as a status symbol when financially they could not afford one. Several other letters and articles in the press around this period expressed the view that many domestics were expected to work extra time for no extra pay (*Express*, 12 June 1979) and that they were underpaid and underprotected.

Recent Developments in Legislation

Over the last decade, the plight of household workers seems to have been given special consideration in several Caribbean territories. As already hinted, this has taken the form in Trinidad and Tobago, of the establishing of a Minimum Wages Board to propose a minimum wage and fair working conditions for domestic workers. According to this legislation which came into effect in January 1980, household assistants were to be paid a weekly wage of TT$55.00 during 1980 and TT$70.00 during 1981 for a 44-hour work week spread over six days. For the first time, therefore, the working hours of this category of workers had been stipulated. Another first, insofar as the conditions of household workers were concerned, is that they were not required to work on public holidays. Even if they lived in with meals, this was to have no bearing on the stipend proposed by the Board.

By 1982 domestic employees in Trinidad and Tobago were to be represented by their own union, the National Union of Domestic Employees (NUDE), run solely by women and headed by the General President, Clotil Walcott— a long-time fighter for women's rights. Ms Walcott had organized a group of domestic employees and had been agitating for recognition for several years before it was finally gained in 1982. NUDE is now very vocal in the cause of domestic employees in Trinidad and Tobago. The situation of domestics in Barbados is not a favourable one. The one piece of legislation which exists for their protection is the Domestic Employees Hours of Duty Act, which states that a domestic worker should not work more than eight hours a day, except by special agreement with the employer. The employer who breaks this law will be fined BDS$25.00. In 1982 there was no legislation fixing a minimum wage for domestic employees.

The situation in Guyana is similar. Little or no legal protection exists for domestic workers. By 1979, Guyana had enacted no minimum wage agreement for domestic workers. The minimum wage which then applied to other categories of work—that of G$11.00 per day—did not apply to domestic workers. It is useful to note the history of domestic workers' struggle in Guyana. As far back as 1922, the Labour Union led by Hubert Critchlow had agitated for improved working hours and minimum wages for domestics; in 1948 the colonial government appointed a committee to look into the working conditions of domestics and persons in the catering trade. Later, women militants such as Janet Jagan attempted to get domestics unionized, and ten years later, when the People's Progressive Party was in office, the Domestic Workers' Union was a registered body. For the past two decades, however, this Union has been defunct.

In Jamaica, a minimum wage rate of 75 Jamaican cents per hour was proposed for household workers by the Jamaica Trade Council to the National Minimum Wages Board, and subsequently a minimum wage stipulation put forward by this Board has been enacted since 1978. At another level, efforts are being made by some Jamaican women in Sistren—a working-class women's theatre group—to highlight the conditions of domestic workers in Jamaica. Two of their staged plays, *Domestick* and *QPH* focus on and pay tribute to "women's work". St Christopher, like Trinidad and Tobago and Jamaica, also has a minimum wage for domestic workers. This wage was set up in June 1974 at EC (Eastern Caribbean) 60 cents per hour with the additional agreement that the total wages for any part of the week should not be less than EC$20.00 per week. (One EC$ = .27 US$).

While the situation of domestic workers appears to be grim in the Caribbean, it is encouraging that some attempt is being made to organize these employees, to raise public consciousness about the value of housework and household workers and, at the state level, to enquire into their wages and working conditions.

Areas of Concern

Four major areas bedevil the situation of domestic workers. The first relates to the attitudes held, both in the society at large and by employers themselves, that domestic workers are less deserving of respect than other workers and that housework is non-work. A change in attitudes towards housework itself and to the labour performed by domestic workers is needed. This could be brought about by more consideration given by those who employ household assistants, with regard to overtime, accommodation and so on. The second area concerns the wages received by domestic workers. These should, in the first instance, be commensurate with the jobs performed by the domestic worker. Minimum wages should also reflect the fact that domestic workers have families to support and need to survive under similar costs of living to those endured by the employer class.

Support services for domestic workers are non-existent. While looking after other people's children, they use makeshift facilities such as elderly relatives to care for their own. Proper day-care or nursery facilities should be provided cheaply for such workers. Finally, there is every need for domestic workers in all the Caribbean territories to become organized. Lessons have to be learnt from the countries in which these workers have already gained union recognition. So far, we have seen that the gains won among domestic workers were made through the efforts of working women themselves. This suggests that any organization among domestic employees has to be spearheaded by women themselves, especially women of the working class; they can best articulate their grievances and propose solutions in their own interests.

Chapter 6: Women and Entrepreneurship

by Jeanette Bell

Introduction

An entrepreneur is essentially a person who owns or controls a business through which income is gained. Here basic market forces are in operation; the entrepreneur makes a profit from a capacity to supply perceived needs. The particular area of activity depends on the skills, abilities and resources available to the individual. Entrepreneurs operate within the formal and informal sectors of our economy. Businesses in the formal sector have reached a stage where a defined social and legal status are advantageous. This status is reflected in the enterprise having a registered name and specific location and in having its nature and scope of business and legal status clearly determined. In the informal sector, on the other hand, the owner/operator is the enterprise. The area of activity and the location are not necessarily fixed and can vary depending on the entrepreneur's judgement. Entrepreneurs operating in the informal sector are not in general accorded high social status. But it has been the starting point for some who have later become part of the formal system.

Caribbean Women's Involvement

Caribbean women have been involved in the economic life of our societies as workers and entrepreneurs throughout our history. From the period of slavery onwards, Caribbean women have combined compulsory labour on the plantations with work on their plots of land to produce food for household consumption as well as for sale on the local markets. Women were the producers as well as the vendors of agricultural produce and handicrafts. Emancipation brought freedom in a technical sense; but in reality the limited opportunities available meant that the majority of the working population was obliged to remain as low-wage-earners on the plantations supplementing income from local production and sales.

With the growth of the public sector and the settlement of a small immigrant, commercial sector (Europeans, Jews, Asians, Chinese and Syrians), there was a need for an increasingly educated professional and clerical class. This middle class was more urban-based and in turn provided an impetus for the growth of small-scale enterprises to meet the needs of this sector.

Women engaged in trading agricultural produce and other kinds of small-scale vending and retailing and provided services such as dress-making, hairdressing, catering and handicraft production. The men set up barber's and tailor shops, or were carpenters, joiners, masons and retailers of liquors and 'dry foods'.

Entrepreneurship provided an opportunity to gain economic independence at a time when educational and employment opportunities were limited for the majority of the population. The small elite who were able to benefit from the opportunities available were being groomed for more prestigious employment not only in the traditional professions of medicine, law and teaching, but also as civil servants and clerks.

The large number of women—approximately 40%—who shouldered sole responsibility as heads of households were highly motivated to use their entrepreneurial skills to provide for their families and educate their children, since education was acknowledged to be the major factor in social mobility.

Entrepreneurship did not, for these women, necessarily require heavy capital outlay. Relatively small amounts could be invested in stock, which in turn would provide more funds for further investment while at the same time profits would help in meeting family expenses. Setting-up funds came from personal savings or were borrowed from members of the family or through indigenous banking schemes such as "meeting turns", "partners", or "Su-Su".

Entrepreneurship not only brought economic independence to these women but also gave them more power in decision-making within the home and in their relationships with their male partners. Despite its low status in the wider society, it provided needed goods and services and brought some status to the entrepreneur as well as the ability to provide for herself and family. The formal and informal sectors existed side by side. The formal sector has expanded while the informal has remained small and peripheral—for a variety of reasons.

Traditional Values/Lack of Recognition

Women gained skills and confidence in a very practical way through "hands on" experiences. However, the need to provide for self and family limited the extent to which finances could be reinvested in the business. The low social status of entrepreneurship meant that women often had more conventional ambitions for their children—a good education and entry into the middle-class professions of law or medicine—rather than wishing them to carry on the business.

Lack of access to credit, because of the policies and practices of lending institutions requiring collateral and guarantors, meant that entrepreneurs operating in the informal sector did not qualify for loans. This lack of access was compounded by women's own reluctance to borrow and risk losing their meagre resources. This meant that while established businesses had access to resources and could expand, the small-scale operators remained small.

Collective efforts, such as savings schemes, worked quite satisfactorily; but in many cases women preferred to operate independently in the actual conduct of business and assume full responsibility for management. Associations of business women have been virtually unknown until recent times in the Caribbean.

This sector of enterprising women has faced increasing competition from each other as well as from formal sector enterprises which in some cases adopted similar strategies to those of the informal sector—such as credit sales to retail customers. Government policies of industrialization by invitation meant that foreign capital was attracted and that the industrial estate and production became a reality. Many of these enterprises, which are large by Caribbean standards, took over production in areas in which women had traditionally had a foothold, such as garment production and food processing. Direct linkages between the plantation owners and the commercial sector— the supermarkets—have eroded the traditional role women have played in marketing food and other produce.

Strategies for Change

Since International Women's Year in 1975, followed by the UN Decade for Women 1976-85, there has been a far greater awareness of the contribution that these women have and continue to make in our societies. Demands are now being made for more opportunities for women and for more women to take up the opportunities available for education and training. Greater access to credit and necessary support services are now being seen as critical for women entrepreneurs operating in the informal sector. Many initiatives have been taken at individual level as well as collectively. Community/collective enterprises have started in traditional as well as non-traditional areas. But if these initiatives are to succeed a long term commitment is needed at all levels and across all relevant sectors.

Reorientation
There is a need to re-examine our strategy and tradition of producing then selling and to look at one where production is guided by up-to-date and accurate information on market demands and trends. There is need also to question and reassess our traditional beliefs. Is there more strength and potential in collective rather than in individual efforts? When and how can women gain from greater organization?

Research Information
Marketing research, information gathering and dissemination to production units is invaluable. So is feasibility analysis prior to the implementation of income-generating projects and other economic enterprises for women.

Collaboration and Support

Where Standards Institutes exist or facilities are available these services should be made available to women and be used to ensure high quality of production. Suitable training organizations should be identified to provide appropriate management and human relations training at convenient times and locations, and at levels that are relevant to the needs of women trainees.

Supportive Policies and Legislation

Policies should encourage and stimulate local entrepreneurship and promote the use of local resources to increase self-sufficiency and export potential, rather than placing such a heavy emphasis on external resources and imports.

Resources

Not only financial, but also human resources are necessary to provide adequate follow-up, monitoring, counselling and on-the-job training for women entrepreneurs.

With these kinds of policies, resources and supportive systems, the entrepreneurial spirit demonstrated by Caribbean women over the last two centuries can be encouraged and can continue to flourish in a climate that is more sensitive and responsive to the interests and needs not only of the individual entrepreneur but of the individual countries in the region.

Chapter 7: Women in Small-Scale Economic Enterprises

by Annette Isaac

Introduction

While there are specific constraints that prevent women from participating in the economy, it is well recognized that women play an indispensable role in the development of Caribbean economies. Lack of comprehensive data has, however, hampered efforts to gauge the real extent of their contribution to the economic and social productivity of the region.

Employment opportunities for women have increased over the years but they are mainly in low-skilled, low-paying positions. With the decline in agriculture and a slowing down in hiring in the public and private sectors, an increasing number of women have turned to the informal sector both for wage and self-employment. Unofficial estimates put the number of women participating in this sector at 30%. These women are usually involved in a broad range of micro-retail and service activities whose remunerative potential it is often difficult to determine. It is generally acknowledged, however, that the informal sector in which Caribbean women predominate forms the backbone of the local economy. It is also known that the informal traders in particular make a significant contribution to the trade consumer sectors at the national level even though GDP figures persistently underestimate their real value and contribution.

Lately much attention is being focused on the informal sector because of its resilience to the current economic depression and its ability to provide jobs and generate income for women and youth who are most affected by lack of employment opportunities.

Small-scale Enterprises in the Formal Sector

The percentage of women independently owning or operating businesses in the formal sector is small. There are, however, a number of women in partnership businesses with their husbands or other family members. This relationship differs from that of women in similar arrangements in the informal sector since those in the formal sector have more decision-making power, are paid full salaries and are very often responsible for handling the financial and

51

legal matters of the businesses. Women within this sector usually live in urban areas. They have had secondary or higher education and several years experience or training in the particular field of business. They usually have few problems in obtaining credit or in dealing with bank managers; they are familiar with market technology and have a good understanding of market operations. These women also have access to day-care facilities and receive support from spouses and other relatives.

These women are involved in businesses such as travel agencies and car rentals, restaurants, small hotels and guest houses, jewellery manufacturing and boutiques. The difficulties that they encounter are those faced by all enterprises in this sector. There is no clearly defined government policy, incentives scheme or protection for small-scale enterprises. The shortage of skilled or trained junior and middle management staff, and the difficulties of obtaining adequate loans (even by customers whose credit rating is good) are key factors that affect the success or otherwise of these ventures.

Small-scale Enterprises in the Informal Sector

It is important to recognize at the outset that within the informal sector many of the problems faced by lower-class women apply equally to men. This is especially so with regard to collateral for loans, and to levels of education and skill. The predicament of all informal entrepreneurs is a very complex one affected by myriad social, economic and political forces; to identify the specific problems of women in this sector is therefore not straightforward.

Of the estimated 30% of the female working population involved in productive activities in this sector, the majority are clustered at the lowest levels. Here they are involved in very micro-activities, both in scale and earnings, and in fact operate far removed from the reality of the business world. Their activity is very often used to supplement other income from part-time employment or remittances from abroad. Many of these micro-businesses therefore have a definite lifespan; as soon as the activity has fulfilled a particular financial need, the transient entrepreneur drops out.

There is a distinction in the kinds of activity in which women in the informal sector are engaged. One type can be described as commercial, the other as developmental. The first category is comprised of individual, family and cooperative enterprises, the sole motive of which is to create employment and generate income. The majority of these activities are self-sustaining.

The developmental type enterprise is more complex. It is often organized and managed by two or more women, is usually community based and is principally geared towards the provision of community services. It provides a source of income for the women (usually a mix of employed and unemployed) in the sense that once the community expenses are taken care of, the remaining money may be divided equally among group members. Partly because of their community orientation, the great majority of these enterprises are not entirely self-supporting, but receive grants or loans from various funding agencies.

This type of business has good employment potential, but because its basic purpose and objectives are *not* commercial, it disintegrates when women find employment elsewhere.

The majority of women in the informal sector live in poor urban or rural communities. A high percentage are heads of households who in many cases are the sole income-earners in their families. Basically they have had only a primary education, and little, if any, training in marketable skills. Because of this they cannot readily find employment in the formal public or private sectors. Usually they do not have a fixed place of business and may move from one spot to another to "catch customers". On the whole they are engaged in traditional activities, they do not usually keep records of their transactions and they experience great difficulty in dealing with and obtaining credit from the formal banking system. These women rely almost solely on the extended family system for help with child-care, since they do not have access to, or cannot afford to pay for this service. These women are engaged in a wide variety of businesses including basket-making and weaving, dress-making, furniture production, pottery, wine-making, food preparation and preservation, shopkeeping, running snackettes and small bars, livestock and vegetable production, hairdressing and huckstering/trafficking, among others.

Problems Facing Women in the Informal Sector

The entrepreneurs of these micro-businesses experience great difficulties in obtaining loans even from financial institutions designated for small businesses such as development banks and local foundations. Many of them do not have the necessary collateral as they do not own land or property. In other cases married women wanting loans are still required to get their husband's signature before a loan is granted—even when the collateral is in both names. Some do not and have never used the commercial banks and therefore do not have established credit ratings; and for those who do use the banks their level of savings is often too low to be used as security.

Many small entrepreneurs, especially in rural areas, are mistrustful of banks and prefer to borrow from local money-lenders or relatives who can supply them with *small amounts* of *quick and ready* cash and with a great deal more privacy. Banks have fostered this attitude themselves by their exorbitant collateral requirements, high interest rates and total absence of structures to respond to the needs of the small business sector. Where loans have been secured from NGOs, problems have been encountered in the management of the funds and this has led to erratic repayment and related problems. (It must, however, be stressed that women have a better track record than men in repaying loans.) The non-existence of credit institutions which cater for and respond to the needs of these really micro-enterprises adversely affects their scope, level of operation and their success or failure.

Women are concentrated in these informal sector activities because of the lack of career options and choices for women in the lower income brackets, the lack of opportunities for continuing education and skills training and the traditional attitudes which still exist towards women's roles in the society. Functional illiteracy is a reality for many rural women especially in countries where two languages are spoken (in Dominica and St Lucia, French patois/Creole is the common spoken language, but English is the official language). The lack of educational and training programmes through which women can acquire skills are responsible for the low level of such skills among women in this sector. At the same time, the absence of structures or the malfunctioning of existing structures prevent women from obtaining access to the necessary resources. Their ability to produce in response to real demands or to increase their level of production is limited and ultimately prevents them from generating sufficient income or accumulating profits.

At another level, the absence of adequate day-care facilities and other support services does not allow them to function at high production levels. Women's multiple roles prevent them from having either the energy or the time to devote to prolonged periods of training or to skill improvement programmes. Poor women often lack the motivation and self-confidence to get ahead in business, though this constraint is a result of their low social and economic status in the society.

Issues for Consideration

A close interrelationship between sectoral issues and those specific to women is more apparent within the informal sector where variables such as education, wealth and status heavily influence women's successful participation in small-scale enterprises. The informal *micro*-sector has potential for greatest impact on women in terms of employment and income creation. However, this potential has to be weighed against such factors as the skills of the population (critical in the case of women), the (future) development of industrial estates which tend to absorb low-skilled labour and the presence and availability of job counselling and training programmes.

The greatest need of women in small micro-enterprises is for training and credit.

Training Programmes provide the most effective ways of addressing many of the problems faced by women in this sector. Training should be at two levels—classroom and on-the-job. In both cases training for these women must be sustained and long term.

Credit: special facilities such as small loan windows, should be set up at existing financial institutions to respond to the credit needs of micro-business women and men. Intermediary institutions such as National Development Foundations should be considered as a *real* alternative to channel credit and technical assistance to the micro-business sector.

There is an immediate and urgent need for further in-depth investigation and data gathering on small-scale enterprises, especially in the informal sector. Specific data is required on the size and characteristics of small businesses, on the needs and motivation of women (and men) who participate in this sector and on the *real* extent of their economic contribution to the overall economy. This need for accurate and precise data on women in this sector can be met by monitoring existing and on-going social and household surveys, sectoral studies and research projects on women. In addition, government and other agencies should sponsor and encourage micro-studies on specific groups of women so as to gain deeper insights into the factors that enhance or retard their participation in the national economy.

Finally, economic planners in the region must begin to take seriously not only the fact that women do make a significant economic contribution to the economics of the region, but that a significant number of women are doing so because of their involvement in small-scale economic enterprises, especially in the informal sector.

Chapter 8: The Hucksters of Dominica

by Hannah Clarendon

Introduction

As far back as the 1930s hucksters were operating in Dominica and are still a very important link in the market chain. They make contact with both producers and consumers. They buy their produce from farmers and travel to other islands to sell it to overseas clients. Originally they were involved in transporting and selling citrus fruit in Barbados and in the French Islands of Martinque and Guadeloupe. Indeed many of the women in the marketplace in Barbados today are Dominican hucksters who did not return home; and we still have in our midst women who braved the seas on all kinds of schooners and in all kinds of weather conditions trying to make a living.

In those days apart from being a housewife, housekeeper or a field-hand, a woman had little opportunity to be an independent person. Huckstering had always been the one area where a woman could organize herself, acquire some dignity and at the same time be economically independent. Hucksters have always been hardworking. They managed their loads with little help from men. Most of their packing was done near the home or at the side of the road. On the outgoing trip they carried agricultural produce and on the return trip they brought home dry goods which they retailed from their homes or at the roadside in trays.

Pre-Hurricane David in 1980 there were many more of these women in the 35-50 age group. This is significant, for there was a time in 1978 when the trade was at a really low level; there were many shops in town, more hotels and the Sun Style Service Garment Factory employed younger women. Before Hurricane David, the French authorities decided to make it more difficult for people going to Guadeloupe and the hucksters had to show 1,500 francs before they were allowed to enter the country. This curtailed their activities somewhat as money was scarce. In the early 1970s there was a great deal of trade with the US Virgin Islands, but towards the end of the decade there was a serious decline with as little as 20 tons of produce going weekly. During this same period trade with Barbados and Martinique slowed somewhat, perhaps because of fewer schooners calling, of immigration problems and changes in market demands.

Since Hurricane David and the closing of some business outlets in town, more and younger women (20-35 years) are unemployed. When many women lost their jobs at hotels and shops, one of the options open to them was self-employment; becoming a huckster was one of the easiest avenues open to them. There was no money in circulation so it did not make sense trying to open a business in Rosseau; the idea was to go where the money was.

Characteristics of the Huckster Trade

The women either get organized with a little working capital and buy a couple of bags of produce or get credit for it from farmers. They then go to the shipping agent, pay for a ticket and freight, get warrants prepared and their goods declared on the ship's manifest. At customs they present the warrant, pay for wharfage at the port and get a phytosanitary certificate—which they must have at all cost even though they may not always understand why! Having made all of the declarations, got a visa and the amount of money required by the country they intend to visit, they are ready for the voyage.

When they arrive at the overseas port, they unload their produce, pass through customs, pay the required duty and leave with their goods. They make their way to the market-place where over the next two days they sell their produce. Most of the transactions, packing and handling are carried out by the women themselves. They go to the countryside and make contact with farmers to buy produce and they often pay for it even before they receive it. They do all of the trafficking around town to get the various documents—they dare not forget any of the papers and they had better get them in order or they may spend days going around in circles. They must also have a return plane or boat ticket.

Packing of produce usually takes place near hucksters' homes or on the roadside nearby. In some cases children and other relatives may help with loading, unloading and packing. Often there is no shelter for the produce which begins to come in on the day before the boat sails and may continue up until the time of leaving.

If we follow these hucksters to the other islands, we notice that the majority of newcomers sit in the market-place whereas most of the older experienced ones have built up contacts and deliver their produce to buyers immediately. When their goods have all been sold, the women buy dry goods such as soap, peas, potatoes, plastic-ware and some fancy ornaments which they take back home to sell. Their standard of living has not shown any marked improvement—they are simply making ends meet.

Problem Areas

The women in this trade are faced with a number of problems—immigration, quality control, unsuitable storage facilities on the boats, lack of marketing information, lack of suitable packing and storage facilities prior to shipping and lack of insurance coverage for their goods.

Hucksters need visas to enter certain countries in the region such as Guadeloupe, Martinique, French St Marten and the US Virgin Islands. To obtain a visa, especially for the French countries, is difficult as the procedures are not standardized. A visa is issued only for three months whereas the hucksters' licence is issued for one year. To get to the US Virgin Islands, a huckster has to be recommended by another *bona fide* huckster before she can get a business visa. She also has to show a certain amount of money. In addition, renewal of passports ($20.00 EC) is expensive and the passport itself is used up very quickly because the huckster needs to make many journeys to other islands.

As hucksters are in a rush most of the time they have little time to check on the quality of the produce that they receive and more often than not it is of poor quality. Farmers sometimes pick fruit in the rain or pick it several days before so that it is in a semi-deteriorated state. They may then mix it with fresh fruit to fool the huckster. Root crops are sometimes delivered with a lot of soil on them and the huckster ends up paying for at least 10lb of soil per 100lb-bag of produce delivered. The actual arrangement to buy produce is a very loose one. Hucksters go to the country and make contact with the farmers to have produce delivered but are never sure that it will be delivered until they actually receive it. There is no organized place at which to receive the ordered goods and at most times they are simply delivered at the roadside. Prices are not controlled and hucksters may pay anywhere between $15.00-30.00 for a crate of limes at any one time. Because there is so much competition during periods of scarcity, the hucksters themselves allow the farmers to sell them anything at any price. At other times, the farmers realize that they cannot get away with the poor quality produce, but they have got used to supplying goods of poor standard. There is a high rate of spoilage as the type of packing material used is not always suitable for the produce, most of which is packed in hemp or plastic bags. Produce is often severely damaged on the boat. Most of the boats are not designed to carry agricultural produce and there is overheating and mechanical damage to the produce in the hold of the ship. Bad handling by the packers and loaders who are not trained to handle this type of produce, poor transport arrangements and inadequate storage facilities all affect the quality of the produce.

Quality control is the most critical problem, since there is no standardization in the type and quality of packing material. Hucksters have become used to taking any kind of ungraded produce and because the need has been there and they had no competition in the islands, there has been no incentive for them to pack and grade their produce better. However, with hucksters from other producing islands coming into the market, the hucksters in Dominica can now only make money when things are really bad on the other islands.

The absence of proper packing material and storage space on the island is also a part of the problem as high costs usually make it unavailable to the hucksters. Packing is done in bags and large wooden boxes holding two to three hundred fruits. Fruit and vegetables are not washed and little or no selection or grading is done.

There is also a total lack of marketing information except for what the hucksters surmise for themselves. There are no regulations on the amount of produce that leaves the country and this varies according to the size of the market at different times of the year. Hucksters lose a lot of money because of lack of information about market demands. The result is that commodities can be bought for unreasonable prices and resold for much less. Each trip is risky and hucksters have no idea whether or not they will make any profit; as a result many have been forced out of the trade. Each huckster currently bears the total cost of stolen articles and damage suffered during the loading and unloading; because insurance rates on perishable commodities are so high, she often cannot afford to pay the premiums. Even when boats go adrift and goods are lost, or bad weather forces the captain to unload, the huckster pays for it all.

Economic Importance of the Huckster Trade

There has never been any doubt that the huckster trade is an important one. What was not clear was whether or not the small farmers were important. However, with the increasing interest in small farmers, the growing of domestic crops and marketing outlets for them have become critical. But because there are no organized market outlets for these crops small farmers are dependent on the hucksters for marketing their crops. The local Marketing Board does not absorb all of the produce from the small farmers and it is left to the hucksters to absorb the extra grapefruit, limes, mangoes, avocado pears and other food crops. It is very difficult to obtain accurate information on the actual amounts that are absorbed by the hucksters who avoid giving correct amounts either to the shipping agents to avoid paying high freight rates, or at the port to avoid high wharfage and port dues. Collecting this information from phytosanitary certificates is also difficult; the figures obtained are often below the real value of the goods.

The Cooperative Citrus Growers' Association depends on hucksters to handle all fruit that is not disposed of in the short season they enjoy on the European market. Not only citrus, but root vegetables and the new tree crop projects will also depend on the hucksters to market whatever produce does not sell on the European market. The huckster trade now extends from Venezuela in the south to St Thomas in the north and involves boats, schooners, canoes and aircraft.

About five hundred (500) persons are involved in the trade; of these about 80% are women and about two hundred (200) are fully employed in this way. Over one thousand persons are dependent on this trade. Figures for 1980 show an increase in production of domestic crops after Hurricane David. Trade figures from the French Departments of Martinique and Guadeloupe show about EC$2 million from the hucksters trade, generated mainly from the sale of agricultural produce. Approximately EC$3 million is earned by the huckster trade annually.

Some Suggestions and Areas for Consideration

Hucksters should have access to marketing information to find out what the market requires. There should be some way of relating a quantity of goods leaving the country to market demand so that any one huckster does not end up losing too much on one trip. In this way, good prices for what was sold would be guaranteed, time would be saved and losses cut down.

The Ministry of Agriculture should institute a system for the inspection of produce and lay down guidelines for packing materials. The hucksters could then purchase the recommended material through an association or the Marketing Board. Inspections should be carried out at the packing site and the conditions under which produce are harvested, packed and transported, sorted, selected and stored should be checked to ensure that they meet the basic requirements. Farmers, packers, handlers and the hucksters themselves should be educated about the proper handling of perishable produce.

There should be storehouses at key locations where produce could be properly stored before leaving the island. Such storehouses would be useful both to farmers and hucksters before and after the final packing is done. They should be well equipped with cooling units to cut down on the field heat and slow down the ripening process. At the same time improvements will have to be made on the boats to make them more suitable for carrying agricultural produce.

All hucksters should be registered and should carry an identification card. The Ministry of Agriculture should recommend *bona fide* hucksters to obtain visas for the U.S. Virgin Islands and the French Islands. The Ministry of External Affairs should approach the French consul to clarify problem areas since hucksters experience great difficulty in actually getting a visa. According to reports there is a lot of preferential treatment and no standard procedure for obtaining a visa. Forms must be paid for on each application every three months and then the forms must be photocopied. Visas should run concurrently with the licences and, like them, should be valid for one year. Hucksters should receive preferential treatment and everything should be done to facilitate their trip.

Technical assistance should be provided to hucksters by way of training programmes. Training could cover simple accounts and book-keeping, handling of produce, proper packing and storing. The Ministry could coordinate this training and coopt the necessary resource persons. Financial assistance should be made available to provide the hucksters with working capital to buy produce and packing material as well as to construct small service sheds and to pay others for their service rendered in packing and loading.

The Hucksters' Association

The successful continuation of the huckster trade depends on the formation of an association through which they can bargain, set up marketing standards and enforce necessary rules and regulations. An association could purchase on behalf of its members and negotiate with government and other financial institutions.

Efforts have recently been made in this direction. A draft constitution was drawn up for the formation of an Association and was ratified at a general meeting of hucksters on 29 June 1981. At the first Annual General Meeting on 27 July 1981 an Executive Committee was elected. It comprises four women and two men.

The general aims and objectives of the Association are:
1. To promote the interests of the Hucksters.
2. To secure financial and technical assistance for its members.
3. To secure proper packing material.
4. To provide general services such as the education of its members; and storage facilities.

The formation of this Association is seen as a major stepping stone for the trade. It is the first of its kind to be formed in the Caribbean. The Association has already made requests to the Ministry of Agriculture for technical assistance to find out the best type of packaging material and its quality, about improved methods of handling, investigating shipping conditions and making recommendations for their improvement. The huckster trade has vast potential not only in terms of earning badly needed foreign exchange, but for creating employment for a large sector of unemployed persons, especially women, in Dominica.

Chapter 9: Caribbean Women and the Trade Union Movement

by Barbara Gloudon

"Executive positions in the trade unions in the Caribbean are still held largely by men, by a ratio of 75 per cent men to 25 per cent women." This information from a 1979 report by the International Labour Organization (ILO), based on a study of nearly 200 trade unionists in executive posts, confirmed what had been known informally all along . . . that although women have been involved in the trade union movement in the Caribbean from its genesis in the 1930s, the positions of power are held by men. The cause and the effects of this imbalance were examined by participants at a regional seminar for women trade unionists held in November 1979 and sponsored by the ILO, the Danish International Development Agency, the Caribbean Congress of Labour, and the Norwegian Federation of Labour.

One of the findings which came out of this seminar was recognition of the absence of leadership training for women in the Caribbean trade union movement. It was acknowledged that women throughout the region were becoming increasingly involved in social and political development and that the time had come to extend a similar level of involvement to the trade union movement.

Arising from the seminar came the Project for the Development of Caribbean Women in Trade Unions, a three-year programme funded by the Inter-American Foundation of Washington DC, and administered by the Trade Union Education Institute of the University of the West Indies' Extra-Mural Department. The Project, which began in 1982, aimed at addressing those problems which have held back women from leadership roles within the trade union movement. This involves the need for skills in management, organization and planning, as well as the need for consciousness-raising both for men and women within the movement, and the need to help women focus on those factors which hinder or promote their personal development as women, workers and citizens.

The Project's schedule included a series of regional seminars which brought together, at intervals, some forty women representing the trade unions and affiliated organizations across the Caribbean. These seminars, held in different locations, helped the participants to gain first-hand knowledge of the distinctive circumstances of each island, and relate them to the regional environment. The seminars also allowed the participants to study trade unionism, social, political and economic developments and involved them in issues connected with personal growth.

From the regional seminars, the programme moved to national seminars conducted by participants in their home territories. At that level, other women in the movement were introduced to the Project and its objectives. In turn, this group conducted local seminars for other women in order to pass on knowledge and skills. By the time the Project ended in 1984, some 2,000 women in the movement had been reached.

The Project was a highly significant initiative for women in Caribbean trade unions. It sought to help women find a way out of a situation into which they have been locked by their own historic, negative attitudes and those of their male counterparts. This is why the question continues to be asked: Why so few women in executive positions in trade unions?

"Because of the macho image of the general secretary", said a leading Trinidad and Tobago jurist recently, while addressing a session of the fourth regional seminar of the Project in Port of Spain. This reply acknowledges the power of the "boss" in the traditional union executive structure, the man in charge of administration and organizing, a "man's man," "one of the boys"—knowledgeable, street-wise, able to command loyalty and affection, "macho".

"Macho? Of course. Every general secretary I know has devoted female followers", said one trade unionist. "You women had better accept it. That is a man's job, women can't be expected to fire one with the fellows in the field [drink with the boys] and, let's face it, that's where a lot of the action takes place. I know you're all liberated but it doesn't work that way". This man's views are not unique. In the experience of the women in the Project, this kind of statement is heard all the time. It goes along with, "What is a nice girl like you doing involved with trade unions? That is for men".

In his message to the opening of the fourth regional seminar of the Project, Errol Mahabir, Trinidad and Tobago's Minister of Labour, said:

> While in no way seeking to ignore the fact that two of the larger trade unions in Trinidad and Tobago elected women trade unionists to the top position of president of their respective unions, it is quite true to say that trade unionism is a male-dominated sphere of activity, and has been so even in those unions which have quite considerable female membership.

The question of women's own perception about their role in the unions was specifically addressed through the Project. In the Project considerable time was spent helping the participants to look at themselves more closely and to examine those traditionally negative attitudes which hinder personal development. Others, men among them, also helped the women to look at their situation.

At the second regional seminar in Nassau, Bahamas, in June 1983, Leonard Archer, President of the Bahamas Union of Teachers—who described himself as fully identifying with the aspirations of women to hold equal status with men—challenged the group to examine their potential for achievement.

"Women in the trade union movement are restricted only in so far as they restrict themselves", he said. "Some women shy away from leadership roles because of an ancient stereotype of women's roles". The situation becomes paradoxical when an examination of the history of the Caribbean trade union movement shows that women played pivotal roles in the critical years of the 1930s, at the movement's turbulent birth. Almost every island has its trade union heroine or heroines, women who gained fame in the movement by providing the support for the men to "go into battle".

In the Jamaican movement, for instance, Aggie Bernard became a legend when she undertook to feed the thousands of men engaged in the waterfront strikes of the late 1930s to early 1940s. In St Kitts, you will hear of the exploits of a woman remembered as "Maggy" whose support role was critical at the time of the 1935 sugar estate campaigns. Research will produce evidence of other women of similar courage throughout the region, proving that there has been no lack of women's involvement in the movement. But the question remains: Why so few leadership roles today?

When Dr Edwin Jones of the UWI Department of Government at Mona addressed the first regional seminar of the Project in Kingston, Jamaica, he noted that trade union women—as indeed other women in the society—in seeking to move forward, needed to examine their historical roles in the Caribbean. Within the labour movement itself, he said, because of the competition for scarce resources, women had become the most exploited among workers, being prepared to accept lower wages and having lower job expectations. He reminded that women were also given the least opportunity to broaden their skills, responsibilities and initiatives at the work-place.

"This is particularly ironical when you consider the situation of women employed by trade unions", says Clive Dobson, a senior officer of Jamaica's National Workers Union.

> I have to admit that while we have made some strides, we are a long, long way off from the situation where women move through the ranks of trade union leadership with the same facility as men. I know of many fantastic women within the trade unions, women who are extremely competent, work hard and get things done. Yet, sad to say, when the time comes to look for an organizer or such position of responsibility the tendency is to turn to the men. We have to change that.

An executive of Jamaica's oldest trade union, the Bustamante Industrial Trade Union (BITU), points out that many women shy away from taking on certain responsibilities because of their multiple roles as home-maker, worker and supporter of the community; so, when the time comes to move up in the unions, some women seem unable to commit themselves to finding the additional time for further responsibility. He however acknowledges the tremendous strength and power in the women of the movement, and points with pride to the achievement of a member of the BITU, Edith Nelson, who was for many years General Secretary and the liaison with one of the most powerful arms of the union—the waterfront workers. But there is a long way to go.

Increased training for leadership is but part of the process, Trinidad's Errol Mahabir admits:

> While women's participation in trade unions has shown some increase, the participation still tends to be in subsidiary rather than in essential positions. For example, their services are more often utilized in the areas of recreational activities and social welfare, while being noticeably lacking in the areas of trade union education and administration.

There are exceptions to the rule. A number of women have emerged in the executive structure of unions and/or affiliated organizations. In Jamaica, Marva Phillips of the Trades Union Congress (TUC) commands respect not only for her role in the TUC administration, but as the only female member of the Board of the Joint Trade Unions Research Development Centre which brings together Jamaica's four major unions in an institution for education and research. She was chosen by her colleagues at the 1979 seminar to become Coordinator for the Project.

In St Lucia, Albertina Phillips was recently elected first vice-chairperson of the St Lucia Workers Union, the first time a woman has reached that level within the organization. In Antigua, Ethlyn Winter is an executive member and trustee of the Antigua Trades and Labour Union. And, in Guyana, Mary Ann Schmidt of the Agricultural and Allied Workers Union is an executive member of the Guyana Trades Union Council.

Trinidad and Tobago's trade union history lists the names of Ursula Gittens, the first woman president of the Trinidad and Tobago Public Services Association, and Daisy Crick, who headed the powerful Women's Auxiliary of the Oilfield Workers Trade Union. Among present-day figures there is Marjorie Wilson of the Union of Commercial and Industrial Workers—a woman of overwhelming strength who uses her humour to mask the seriousness of some of the battles in which she has engaged on the picket line and in confrontation with management. But beneath the humour lies an iron will and a sound grasp of the nature of the challenges which face women in the unions. "We have to be militant", she stresses. "More is demanded of us because we are regarded as new to the task. We can work and work well and we have to continue to get trained to do the work. And remember—one for all and all for one." Marjorie Wilson and her colleagues across the region know that they have chosen no easy path. However, they can take comfort in the fact that others recognize the nature of the task to which they have committed themselves.

Prof. Rex Nettleford, Director of the UWI Trade Union Education Institute, and Project Director, has this to say:

> It cannot be over-stressed that the trade union movement is not simply a movement concerned with wages and benefits. It has to do with changing the status of working-class people. Women, with their concerns for family and home, understand the nature of change and what it implies. For that reason, they have a special contribution to make to the development of the trade union movement.

While accepting the challenge to make that contribution, women employed in Caribbean trade unionism look forward to carving new personal paths for advancement within the leadership structure. The Project for the Development of Caribbean Women in Trade Unions has attempted to equip them for the task.

Part 3: Women and the Family

Chapter 10: The Making of Male — Female Relationships in the Caribbean

by Norma Shorey-Bryan

In the Caribbean, as elsewhere, society and environment are constantly changing. Our lifestyles have had to adapt to a society which is becoming increasingly industrialized and commercialized. We are relying less on backyard gardens, family plots and home products to supplement income. The food we eat, the daily rhythm of our lives, our education schedules and job demands have changed considerably over the years.

The changes have affected all aspects of life, including the relationships between men and women and their expectations of each others' roles and responsibilities. The changes in these relationships are not taking place in a vacuum, but within the context of unique historical and cultural situations that have shaped and continue to shape them. We need to be aware that our roles and relationships are linked not only to how we see ourselves as men and women, but are also closely intertwined with our personal goals and values. In dealing with these new roles and relationships, we need to examine closely our social policies, our personal relationships and the way in which we socialize our children, particularly through the family and the educational system.

This paper focuses on the role of the socialization process as a key factor in shaping and reinforcing our institutional and personal relationships and in particular those aspects that affect our roles and relationships as men and women in the Caribbean and ultimately the quality of these relationships and of our lives.

It is well known that a person's attitudes and values are significantly shaped in childhood and adolescence. In the Caribbean we place a high value on instilling in our children attitudes of respect to elders and sharing within families. Yet in other critical areas of life, we frequently fail to examine whether the values we inculcate in children and youth about their adult roles and relationships as men and women are the ones most beneficial to our society today and in the future.

International research encourages us to question our traditional assumptions and stereotypes about male-female roles and behaviour. It encourages us to look more critically at our own cultural setting in the Caribbean. In particular, since the family plays a major role in helping to shape our identity and how we perceive our roles in the society, it is important to review the dynamics of the Caribbean family patterns and interactions. Extensive analyses of family patterns in the Caribbean from various perspectives have identified culture and class as two critical factors which influence family structure and relationships, as is common to all societies. The high proportion (30-40%) of female-headed households indicates that a significant percentage of women in the Caribbean—unlike many other societies—are often the major economic providers for their families. In addition Caribbean women place a high cultural value on mothering and child-care. Women carry the major responsibility for child rearing, but sacrifices made in this area have been traditionally seen as investments for the future. Most women anticipate the satisfaction and prestige of seeing their children "do well" while many also expect and look forward to financial support from children in their old age.

However, since a high percentage of women who work outside the home are employed in low status, low pay jobs in agriculture and in the service sector, they experience a great deal of stress as they try to provide for their families with limited economic resources. Many seek, and often have to fight for, economic support or maintenance for children from the fathers of their children. Information from the Jamaican Family Court indicates that over 70% of the cases brought there relate to problems of obtaining child support from fathers.

Since women's search for economic and emotional security with men is often unsuccessful, Caribbean women have had to develop other ways to cope with their family responsibilities. Coping strategies include support networks where grandmothers, aunties and cousins are available to assist in child-rearing, and even give a "little something here and there" to help out. In-depth interviews carried out with individual women in the Women in the Caribbean Research Project (WICP), emphasized the importance of friendship ties with other women in times of emotional stress and difficulty.

Another important factor affecting the Caribbean family is the absence of men. Although they may be tied to women by marriage or common law, men often play a limited role in family life and child-rearing and in that sense they are 'marginal' to their families. At another level M.G. Smith postulates that male marginality to the family often parallels the economic marginality of the majority of the Caribbean working class to the dominant social and economic structure. Many men who are not physically present may be involved in visiting relationships with several women, all of whom expect financial support from them. The absence of men may be attributed to unstable economic conditions in the Caribbean which force men to leave their families when they cannot fulfil the traditional role of provider. Smith also examines the psychological aspect of male marginality. It is possible that many men feel alienated from their families precisely because they feel a subconscious guilt in not being able to live up to their own, and society's, ideal of being the provider.

This ambivalence which men often face in not being economically strong also affects their self-image; they often feel that they can only bolster their ego by asserting their dominance over women and children. This may be done physically through violence or emotionally as they constrain their women's freedom. Women often attribute their inability to be involved in community affairs—taking up opportunities for further training and education or furthering personal development—to their men's "forbidding them" to go out.

Many men feel that their "macho" image is enhanced when they try to assert control over their women and wives. Yet paradoxically men depend on the very women they despise to bolster their egos and provide emotional support. Although men may recognize this dependency, they also resent and may even fear it, since it is a common belief that a man should always be strong and should never have to depend on a woman.

These are some of the many paradoxes and conflicts inherent in the very nature of the relationships between Caribbean men and women, and which prevent these relationships from being fulfilling and satisfying to both partners. Children observe these patterns of interaction and learn similar patterns of behaviour and attitudes, as they internalize what roles and behaviours are appropriate to their sex. In conducting sessions with a variety of groups of adults and young people in Barbados, Jamaica, Grenada and Dominica, I have often asked them to think about the Ten Commandments which they learned when they were children, on how boys and girls should behave. From their responses, it became clear that the socializing commandments which they received were surprisingly similar, regardless of the age or type of group.

These commandments were related to the tasks they were expected to do in the home: girls to cook, clean and wash; boys to sweep the yard and to take out the garbage. The commandments also specified behaviours and attitudes: girls could cry, boys should not. From all of these commandments children learnt that women and men were expected to play different roles in life. From their observation of adult male-female relationships, children saw women giving and men receiving care and nurturance, but they seldom saw men reciprocating since many men believe that it is unmanly to show their emotions.

At the same time children often observe that the interactions between women and men are dominated by women's constant demand for money. This is one aspect that men resent. Barrow's study on men's attitudes toward women supports the view that many men see women as avaricious and demanding and therefore resent them. Many of the tensions between men and women have their roots in economic issues; but these tensions are also born of social expectations. While men see women as avaricious and demanding, women see men as irresponsible. These negative perceptions affect both the quality of interaction and of male-female relationships.

The socialization process is a circular one. Values and attitudes about male-female relationships taught to children are transmitted to the next generation, since the women themselves consciously or unconsciously teach their children to accept differing behaviours and expectations for men and women. It is unfortunate that children are not often able to experience harmonious relationships between their parents; when they themselves become adults they often do not know how to make the male-female interactions more positive.

The School System

The socialization process continues throughout the school years. Teacher expectations of what boys and girls are capable of doing subtly reinforce traditional assumptions of appropriate male and female roles. From the nursery school where girls are given dolls to develop their nurturing capacity, and boys have trucks and hammers to emphasize mechanical skills, gender differences are reinforced.

In 1975 the Barbados National Commission on the Status of Women expressed its concern at existing curriculum choices and training opportunities at the secondary level and the limited possibilities for boys and girls in the world of work. The Commission noted that mathematics and science were seen to be less important for girls than for boys. So in spite of the fact that in the Caribbean the majority of secondary school graduates are girls, a much smaller percentage of girls were prepared to enter scientific and technological fields. This in itself was seen as a serious factor affecting women's participation in the modern world of technology.

It must be noted, however, that as a result of some critical analysis of the above, specific programmes have been initiated to sensitize teachers, counsellors and curriculum specialists at both primary and secondary levels about the implications of sex-role stereotyping. Some teachers who are now more conscious of these issues have taken deliberate action to create a more balanced environment, and curriculum, for the students.

The development of a new curriculum and textbooks both at the primary and secondary level, through a regional Primary Education Project and the Caribbean Examinations Council, is providing an opportunity, through textbook illustrations, and activity centred research for students, to portray women and men playing a variety of roles. Perhaps in the future, schools in the Caribbean will help students to develop according to their interests and capabilities, rather than by stereotyped expectations of their sex/gender.

School also plays a critical role in preparing young people for future careers. The writer has conducted sessions with both female and male students in the upper forms of secondary school. Students were asked to list and discuss what types of jobs men and women should do. Their typical responses were that men are lawyers, electricians, technicians; while women are teachers, clerks, secretaries and nurses, clearly indicating how completely the students had internalized traditional views on appropriate work for women and men. Through further discussion and analysis, the same students admitted that there was no real reason why boys and girls could not equally well perform a wide range of jobs. For the first time their assumptions about careers for men and women had been challenged. The students began to recognize that boys do have a wider range of choices, but that men are also limited by the traditionally negative attitudes of society towards accepting men in jobs which require sensitivity and nurturing skills.

Talk about equal opportunities for men and women will be meaningless unless there is greater involvement of men in family and home activities. A man's presence provides a better role model to children than his absence. Equally important, men's greater involvement in child-rearing and home-making frees women for other activities outside the home. For if women have to carry the entire burden of child-rearing, caring, and house maintenance, their time and energy for developing themselves and their talents will continue to be limited.

These are the kinds of concerns which move the discussion on a change in relationships between women and men from an academic to a very practical level. Seen in this light, the focus on women moves from being a threatening one to one which will benefit not only men and women, but the entire society. The challenge is to convince both men and women that a change in their relationships is not only possible but beneficial. Some of the changes are already occurring. Some women have become more conscious of the need for a different quality of relationships. They are articulating their dissatisfaction with traditional attitudes that restrict their personal development. On the other hand, some men who have recognized that the present relationships they have with their families are not satisfying are already beginning to make the necessary change and provide new role models for their children.

It is the partnership of men and women working together, with a better understanding and acceptance of each others' strengths and weaknesses, contributions and potentials that will point the way to our youth as we seek for a better quality of life for all.

Chapter 11: Violence against Women

by Stephanie Kamugisha

Crimes of violence against women—rape, incest, assault, sexual harassment—are prevalent throughout the Caribbean. Women are beaten, mentally abused, raped and sexually harassed . . . on the streets, in their workplace and in their homes in practically every Caribbean country. This article will, however, focus on those countries for which figures are available, that is, Trinidad and Tobago, Barbados and Jamaica.

Rape and Wife Beating

Of all violent crimes against women, rape is the one most publicized in the region. In Trinidad and Tobago in the 1970s rape crimes increased, with professional and newspaper commentaries describing the prevalence of rape as a "problem". Lynette Seebaram, a barrister in Trinidad, wrote: "The recent spate of newspaper reports of rape and related sexual offences indicates that this crime of violence against women is on the increase in Trinidad and Tobago". The rape crisis coincided with the temporary "money is no problem" era of petro-dollars and capitalist influence. By December 1977, Trinidad's *Express* newspaper reported the more sinister crime of rape-murder and a series of attacks on children.

In Trinidad and Tobago in 1972, 144 cases of rape were reported to the police. In Barbados in 1978 there were 55 reported cases of rape; in 1979, 23; in 1980; 55; in 1981; 62 and in 1982, as in 1978, 55. Cases of carnal knowledge without consent in Barbados rose from 14 in 1978 to 23 in 1982, and cases of indecent assault rose from 17 to 44 during the five-year period 1978–82. Jamaica recorded some 142 reported cases of rape in 1961, with that number rising to 641 by 1973; in these cases only 296 offenders were apprehended and convicted. Today in Jamaica only one in twenty cases are reported.

There seems to be some connection between crimes of violence against women and poverty, high levels of unemployment and female responsibility for support of children. In the United States, the figures indicate that most rapists are slum dwellers (hence the connection with poverty) from inner city areas. In Trinidad's St George County the same relationship between rape and urban poverty can be seen. In order to understand the living standards and quality of life in St George, the census figures must be supplemented by a description of the material conditions obtaining in some of its sub-communities. St George is a county of great contrasts. It takes in plush, surburban, middle-class areas, as well as areas of poverty.

In this environment; the majority of unemployed males are usually dependants rather than heads of households; the woman in the household is often responsible for the support of the children. The unemployed male may feel inferior and beat the woman. Crimes of violence against women are also common in a single-parent household where the father is absent and the mother has the full job of working and caring for the children. Analysis of the correlation between rape and urbanization has established that a higher incidence of rape occurs in the working-class communities of Trinidad and Tobago. (We must, however, be aware of the problems involved in making assumptions based on police statistics in the case of rape, which is an under-reported crime.)

Dr Ruth Doorbar, a consultant psychologist in Jamaica sees rapists in that society as falling into four categories.

There's a guy who staged a robbery with his cronies and came upon one or two helpless women. His exercise of power, using sex as the vehicle, is an act of bravado, an expression of the power of men. Then, there is the male who feels sexually inadequate, unattractive or sexually inferior, who must validate his manhood by ravaging a young and sexually inexperienced victim. The majority of rapists are to be found among men with deep psycho-neurotic problems. These are, in the main, men who were raised without the presence of a father-figure, developed an early sexual attachment to the mother-figure and were socialized into repressing this sexual feeling. The offenders from this category usually select maternal victims.

Then, there is the boy who grew up with a sense of having been unfairly disciplined or chastised at home. He was always accused of wrong-doing but learned to repress his hostility to this treatment. He became a divided self: wanting approval and affection but fearing that he would be chastised and isolated. Many grow up hating women and see women as objects for sex, food and babies. They are usually the spouse beaters . . . the young baby fathers.

The difference between the professional rapist and the average dominant heterosexual may be mainly quantitative. In Caribbean culture the attraction of the male to violence and death is traditional. Another factor which is evident in our culture is that heterosexual love finds expression through male dominance and female submission.

In the courts today, in some parts of the Caribbean, it is assumed that a woman who does not respect the double standard of sexual morality deserves what she gets. While in some countries a man's previous rape convictions are not considered admissible evidence, the sexual reputation of the rape victim is considered a crucial part of the evidence upon which the court must decide innocence or guilt. According to the double standard a woman who has had sexual intercourse before marriage cannot be raped.

Rape is not only a crime of aggression against the body, it is a transgression against chastity as defined by men. When a woman is forced into a sexual relationship, she has, according to the male ethos, been violated. But she is also defiled if she does not behave according to the double standard—by maintaining her chastity or confining her sexual activities to a monogamous relationship. It should not be assumed, however, that rape can be avoided simply by behaving. Myth has it that only "bad girls" are raped. This is not so; rape can happen to anyone, as several major studies have shown. Research shows that rape victims have not provoked their attack in any way and, since many rapes occur in the victim's home late at night, there is really no way she could have "asked for it".

The problem of rape is deeply rooted in centuries of sexual inequality and male domination, as is another common act of violence against women—wife-beating. Wife-beating occurs for a variety of reasons. An assault may occur if the man comes home and his lunch isn't ready; or it may be the outcome of an argument. But assaults are always very brutal and the plight of the abused woman is usually ignored. Some women; especially those from a high socio-economic group, are ashamed and reluctant to let others know what they are experiencing, which explains why the number of complaints reaching the authorities is minimal. Not only are wives and women in visiting or common-law unions subjected to beatings, but women in dating relationships also experience abuse.

Assaults may occur daily, weekly, or as a monthly ritual—their frequency increasing from year to year. Injuries range from bruises, lacerations, swellings, fractures, concussions, or (in the case of pregnant women) miscarriages. Why do women endure such terror and degradation? In most cases, the woman may not be in a job which allows her to support herself and her children and is thus economically dependent on the man. Having no alternative, she cannot extricate herself from a violent family situation. She may not have the necessary education or training to get a job; she may be unaware of her legal rights.

Professionals tend to view the problem of domestic violence as an individual family upset and not as a major social problem. Laws are technically in place against one human physically attacking another, but they are rarely enforced if the victim and attacker are married. Domestic troubles lead to few arrests; they are regarded by the police as personal problems. In most cases the victim usually drops charges. This happens because she is faced with an indifferent, hostile legal system where procedures are time-consuming, expensive and humiliating—a system that tends to reinforce the husband's view that he has committed no crime.

Sexual Harassment

Like rape or wife-beating, sexual harassment is an issue of power which derives its meaning not from personality or biology, but from a social context of gender roles and, more specifically, women's role, work and functions. A man who always calls a woman co-worker "honey" or "sweetie", who whistles as she walks by, or stares at her breasts when they are talking, is reminding her that she is just a sex object and not to be taken seriously.

A common method of dealing with sexual harassment is to ignore it; but this does not stop it. In the work-place women who complain are made to feel uncomfortable: on the street, the verbal abuse simply gets more abrasive and sickening. Women for the most part react negatively to sexual harassment. Most get angry, some are frightened and a few feel guilty. Many feel self-conscious, powerless and trapped, and experience physical symptons—from loss of appetite to upset stomach, or migraine headaches.

Society continues to view sexual harassment from a double standard. While the sexual harassers are tolerated—"boys will be boys"—the women victims bear the brunt of the blame. Personnel managers, union representatives, human rights agencies, courts and legislators reflect these discriminatory attitudes. Women who seek assistance from these sources to stop sexual harassment are frequently placing themselves at a risk of humiliating indifference, ridicule, or even further sexual harassment and insinuation. Nevertheless, it is important to use these channels wherever possible—they are the only ones currently available.

Incest

In the Caribbean, incest takes place most frequently between father and daughter or step-father and step-daughter. Fathers who commit incest are reportedly characterized as having had an emotionally deprived childhood and chaotic family life, an extreme emotional dependence on their wives and a non-aggressive and ineffectual personality. In addition, they often have an immature sexual orientation and poor sexual adjustment. Many of them have a history of alcoholism. Little wonder then, that these men fulfil their need for power by sexually assaulting the least powerful being in their lives.

Recent research has shown that the average age of the victim at the commencement of incest is between five to eight. In some cases, however, the child may already have entered puberty. Once the incestuous relationship becomes known to other family members it is usually hushed up. Such was the situation in the case of Cherry, now 23-years-old and a domestic worker in Jamaica. She recalls that as a child she was not believed by her mother or female relatives when she reported an incestuous relationship with her father. She says

> Mama never showed her affection even when she was well and papa was always making jokes about his need for sex. I felt sorry for both of them. When mama was ill and I, as the eldest of six children, started to run the house, papa would visit my room at nights. At first, I told him it was wrong but he said he didn't want to hurt mama by going outside. He slept with me for nearly a year before I became pregnant. Mama beat me when I told her who was the father and asked me not to tell anyone.

The relationship may evolve gradually, with the child unable to offer any physical resistance in the face of her father's increasingly aggressive sexual advances. In some cases the child runs away or the relationship may come to the attention of the authorities if she gets pregnant. This form of violence can result in serious confusion for the child over her sexual identity and may lead her to fear her own sexuality. She may exhibit learning difficulties or physical complaints, become a runaway, attempt suicide, or become sexually promiscuous. The role of the mother is difficult, as she would seem to have control over the situation. But it must be understood that the same economic constraints which keep a woman in situations which are abusive for herself also apply to a situation where it is her children who are the victims.

In the Caribbean very few cases of incest go before the court. It is a crime which often only becomes known through rumour. Nevertheless, it is present and has to be dealt with like any other crime against women.

Fighting Back

Solutions to the problem of sexual abuse lie in family life education, the raised consciousness of the society at large, the possible training of special units within the police force and legal reform. Meanwhile there is much that women and women's organizations can do to provide support to the victim of these abuses, as well as to each other. They could set up refuge centres for beaten women, establish rape crisis centres to counsel women on how to deal with the trauma and lobby for a more efficient and speedy legal process.

Some organizations/groups have already started. In Jamaica, for example, the Women's Centre for Adolescent Mothers does attempt to deal with the problems of sexual abuse wherever it encounters them. According to Pamela McNeil, Coordinator of the Centre, incest is their worst problem and one which they attempt to address before placing the girl back in the society. In the case of rape victims, the Centre assists them in rebuilding their self-image and in facing society again; it also arranges, and prepares the girl, for the adoption of her baby at her request. In each area, the Centre attempts to encourage the girls to develop their inner strength, self-respect and dignity to withstand the pressures of poverty.

Other activities on sexual abuse in Jamaica include the establishment of the Women's Resource and Outreach Centre set up by the Committee of Women for Progress. The Centre provides, among a number of services, free legal services to women to help them deal with problems such as sexual harassment and rape and free medical services. The CWP has also initiated a public education programme to raise awareness of the issue of sexual abuse.

In Trinidad, the Concerned Women for Progress are also raising public consciousness. This Group uses the media and public forums to highlight the issue, as well as skits to publicly present dramatizations of rape situations. Other aspects of their campaign include the production of a handbook on rape and violence and a proposed rape crisis centre. The Women's Arm of the National Joint Action Committee has been addressing the issue in their national consultations entitled "The Woman, the Child, and Society"; and the National Commission on the Status of Women has submitted a number of recommendations from its 1981 seminar on domestic violence to the Trinidad Government which has already agreed to donate land for the establishment of a home for beaten wives.

Elsewhere in the region a women's crisis centre to help physically or emotionally abused women has been established in the Bahamas; the St Lucia Social Services Department has prepared a research proposal on domestic violence which, if implemented, could lead to greater assistance to beaten wives from the legal system; and, in Guyana, the Women's Revolutionary Socialist Movement has called for a family court where investigations and hearings of rape offences could be carried out in private.

Added to these efforts, more and more individual women are reporting crimes of violence against their persons and standing up for their rights in court. This is commendable and could reduce the occurrence of these crimes in years to come.

Chapter 12: Silent Crimes against Jamaican Women

by Lorna Gordon

Is there an unprecedented wave of female sexual abuses threatening to engulf and destroy women in the Jamaican society?

Are the daily media reports of rape, incest, divorce on the ground of physical cruelty and the growing number of victim reports circulated through the grapevine, a true indication of increasing prevalence or of increasing freedom to publicly discuss previously closeted behaviour?

The answer to these questions is anybody's guess. For, despite a recent spate of publicity from concerned citizens and female columnists in the press about the frequency and range of abuses being experienced by Jamaican women, the police maintain a news blackout on statistics. There is also a deafening silence from the established Women's Organizations which might be expected to take up the issue.

Medical practitioners who are among the first to see victims after the police feel there has been a definite upsurge in crimes against women, particularly rape and wife battering. They suggest a correlation between this upsurge, the country's precarious economic situation and the build-up of arms in the civilian population.

There is no average rapist, [says one psychiatrist] by the same token there is no average wife or spouse batterer. The men who commit these crimes against women are acting out their feelings of frustration and impotence, induced by the system, against the most available unit of powerlessness within the system, women. For example, what they cannot express to their employer if they are employed and to the wider society, is channeled into expressed hostility against the women and children in their immediate environment.

One high-ranking police official believes that

while many rape cases are not being reported because of fear of retaliation, given the number of guns in the civilian population, publicising those cases reported to the police would only create mass hysteria and damage the country's image.

But individuals and groups have discovered that there are different reasons for sweeping the issue under the carpet. The recently formed Committee Against Sexual Exploitation (CASE) found that while women were willing to discuss their experiences with friends and relatives in the confines of their home, when invited to identify the men and the organizations involved in cases of sexual harassment at the work-place they were reluctant to do so, fearing victimization and loss of jobs.

In rape cases, identification of the offender is critical to the ability of the police to get the matter into court. Yet, as the Assistant Commissioner in charge of the Criminal Investigation Branch, says,

> Most women stop short of doing so, with the result that the police cannot maintain its surveillance of the suspected offender and he is free to roam different areas of the country committing the same crime. Victims brought to an identification parade fear that they will be recognised by the offender or his friends, and that they will be subjected to further harm, but this is not true. They are protected by one-way mirrors.
>
> In the case of spouse battering, most women fail to press charges and there is nothing we can do under the circumstances. The same applies to incest, where the mother, or female guardian refuses to co-operate because of guilt, shame or the fear of retribution.

The victims tell a slightly different story.

May, a 32-year-old business executive, got little sympathy from the police when she reported beating by her husband. "They thought it was a private domestic matter", she said, "although I was ready and willing to press charges. I got the feeling from them that I must have done something wrong and therefore deserved the punishment." Ten years later she was gang raped by six armed men who invaded her home.

> I reported the matter to the police. Absolutely nothing happened, although I was able to give them some leads to help find the suspected offenders. Many months after the incident, I was invited to an identification parade and when I walked into the police station I got the feeling that I was in the enemy camp. I panicked and ran. I wanted to do the right thing but I did not get the feeling of being supported.
>
> My daughter had witnessed the rape and I agonised over the possible consequences of my identifying the persons. I was not reassured by the attitude of the police. It seemed like my sexual past was on trial and I felt just as guilty as the accused. My husband and my psychiatrist have seen me through the trauma.

Marva, a 24-year-old store clerk who was raped at age 13, reports a harrowing experience which convinced her that "there is no one to turn to".

> I have three children by three different fathers. I got this job and boss was very kind at first. He used to beat his wife and she became sick. One day, he told me that he could make my life easier if I was kind to him. I was afraid of losing my job, so when he asked me to work late at nights in the storeroom, I agreed. He used to give me gifts on special occasions, and extra money on my pay. One night he came into the storeroom like an animal. He tore off my dress and raped me. I reported the matter to the police, but he denied everything I said. The police took me to their doctor, a man, and he was crude. I wanted to die.

The sense of powerlessness pervades not only the reported experiences of rape victims, but also the existence of battered spouses and juniors who acquiese to demands for sexual favours on the job for fear of losing the job, the promotion or the recognition of their worth to the organization. Sexual harassment, like rape or spouse battering, is an issue of power which derives its meaning, not from personality or biology, but from a social context of gender roles and more specifically, women's role, work and functions. The fact is that sexual abuses eat away at the core of a woman's being and can contribute to a lowered feeling of self worth.

The woman who is beaten by her husband or lover and who stays in the situation after rationalizing his problems and concerns and the children's welfare; the woman who gives sexual favours in return for job security; and the woman who turns a blind eye to incestuous relationships in the home, are all in the same boat. They lack the self-esteem to fight back.

A consultant psychologist in private practice who has undertaken research into the issue, feels that women must take the initiative to deal with the situation.

> Women must see the problem as happening to women. The incidence of men being abused by men is extremely rare. We have to look within the home environment for the first set of corrective measures. By that I mean women whether mothers, aunts or grandmothers understanding the socialization of our young people. Then, the education system must deal with the manifestations of potential violence, fighting, stealing, truancy. The educational system has freed the Jamaican population to acquire education, but it has not educated them to human sensitivity, respect for human life, courtesy, thus the cycle of violence inherited from the system of slavery is being repeated daily.

In 1961, some 142 cases of rape were reported to the police. By 1973, that number had risen to 641 and of that amount 296 offenders were apprehended and convicted. That increase prompted a government senator in 1971 to say that "one murder was being committed every two and a half days, rape and carnal abuse every sixteen hours, one case of armed robbery every three hours and fifty minutes, and at least one other serious offence against the person every fifty minutes."

While the rate of detection bears no real significance to the frequency with which the crime is committed, or to the number of cases which go unreported, the figures revealed by the police up to 1973, showed a marked escalation in crimes of rape from 1969 into the 1970s. Has the population of rapists increased? Neither the police nor the doctors are sure.

According to the Assistant Commissioner of Police,

> in many instances the same men are committing the acts all over the place, and are able to do so because the cordon of silence among women is perpetuated. What is not understood, is that this same person or persons could be wanted by the police for other crimes such as robbery, arson, etc. The police force hopes to start a survey early in 1982 to pinpoint the nature and extent of crimes in the society. I am sure that in the course of compiling this data, we will begin to detect specific patterns, maybe involving former rape convicts or persons who were suspected or accused of rape, but who were never brought to justice.

There is obviously no one solution to the problem of rape. This may perhaps explain the general silence by men and women in the society, including groups which claim to represent the interests of women. An individual or group feels powerless to tackle the complex nature of the problems of female sexual abuses, the solution to which lies in family life education, the raised consciousness of the society at large, the possible training of special units within the police force and legal reform. The maximum sentence of life imprisonment has not proven to be a deterrent. In the interim, there is much that women can do by way of providing support to each other. They could bond together to set up refuge centres for battered women, establish rape crisis centres to counsel women in how to deal with the trauma and lobby for a more efficient and speedy legal process.

While these efforts may be considered "bandaid" solutions, they have their merits. For in the final analysis, only a strong female constituent voice which declares WAR, a war against rape and other forms of female sexual abuse and a female constituency willing to take action, in spite of the real and imagined risks, can quell the tide of abuses and bring about a just, humane and caring society.

Chapter 13: Family Relations and Support Systems

by Rosalind Saint Victor

GRENADA:	M. cannot find employment in her native island Grenada. She leaves her 10-year-old daughter in the care of her mother and emigrates to Trinidad where she now works as a maid.
	M. writes home regularly and sends part of her paycheque each month. She is also saving towards the day when she can bring her daughter to be with her.
TRINIDAD:	Mother and Father white-collar workers. Father's mother takes care of children while parents are away at work.
ANGUILLA:	Grandmother taking care of three grandchildren. They are the children of a son and a daughter, both of whom are now living and working in the US Virgin Islands.
BARBADOS:	Big sister raising her own children and her younger sister's child as siblings. Her sister was a mother at 15.
TRINIDAD:	Elderly maiden-aunt takes care of her great-nephew during the week, while his mother studies and works.

From island to island, the circumstances, the characters, the ethnic backgrounds may differ. But, woman to woman extended family support in caring for children has been for a basic fact of Caribbean life which cuts across all these differences.

This support, though, has been so much taken for granted, even by those who give and receive it, that most never recognize its importance nor its impact on Caribbean family and society. Ask any of our people, in any of our territories, to identify the support systems on which mothers could rely for help in caring for their children and, invariably, the answer focuses on day-care centres. Only with prompting is family support afforded a similar recognition. Probably it is because "Tantie" or "Granny" are too close to us. Or that we instinctively dismiss the care they provide as being too informal or ad hoc to merit the title of support system.

On analysis, though, that informal, ad hoc care turns out to be supportive in ways which extend far beyond the practical assistance given to mothers in the care of their children. Not only is mother unhampered to participate in the workforce, she also has the opportunity to improve her sense of self through wider participation, further training or education and thus contribute more effectively to her own and her family's qualitative and financial well being. She also has available to her an emotional buffer which deflects and defuses potentially stressful situations.

Recently, in one of our islands, a woman gave away four children in the market-place. She had reached the end of her tether. She could not cope with them—either emotionally or financially. She claimed that if she had to live with them another day she would have lost all control and killed them. This anecdote jars the sensibilities. And it jars precisely because the emotional buffer of woman to woman support would not normally allow such a situation to get so out of hand. For some reason, this woman's support systems had broken down. There was no relative to extend a helping hand; no one to defray the tension of coping with a difficult situation.

Ordinarily a female relative (or close friend) would have intervened at a much earlier stage to relieve the tension by caring for the children and by providing a sympathetic ear for the mother. This assistance might have been temporary, or it might have been more lasting. But regardless of duration, it would have precluded the type of emotional crisis which forced this mother into the market-place. Such assistance is a family obligation. People in extended family systems are not individuals in their own right so much as they are parts of a corporate whole. Ideally, problems as well as joys are shared by all.

Today, as some of our urban families detach themselves from their extended family, they celebrate the concomitant benefit of a new found privacy away from the interventions of relatives. But even as this particular release is heralded, mothers especially are beginning to reel under the burden of the nuclear family being a unit unto itself and "going it alone".

The Caribbean style, woman-to-woman support system eliminates the need for the counsellor or psychologist on whom our North Atlantic urban sisters tend to rely. These female relatives—by listening, by counselling, by intervening, at times by just being there—contribute, in curative and preventive fashion, to the well being of the families they support. Parent-child and mate-to-mate relationships both benefit.

For the family member who provides the care, there may or may not be a monetary reward. There are some who cast aspersions on grandmothers whom they believe resort to taking care of their grandchildren in order to guarantee themselves some measure of financial or nutritional support. But the exchange of goods and services for cash or kind is the foundation of our economic system. Why then is it so distasteful if Granny can be given the opportunity to maintain her dignity by trading her child-care skills for her own maintenance?

Of course, implied at the heart of that criticism is the feeling that Granny's assistance should be motivated by altruistic love for her daughter or son and her grandchildren. But the critics do not take into consideration the fact that Granny's services can hardly ever be traded at their true market value precisely because of the qualitative difference her love makes in the type of care she gives.

Critics aside though, how many times have we seen Granny and other relatives decry an unplanned or unwanted pregnancy even to the point of "throwing out" the mother-to-be and then turn around and provide full support once the baby arrives on the scene? Caribbean mothers and daughters, particularly those of the lower socio-economic levels, have a strong sense of solidarity which transcends even strong differences of opinion or serious transgressions. It is a solidarity nurtured by a mother's desire to have her daughter "turn out better than me". It is a solidarity expressed through Granny's taking care of her daughter's child so that her daughter may be able to improve her status. It is a solidarity based on genuine love.

To Granny, or Tantie and other females who care for their young relatives, there may be another benefit arising from deep-seated ego needs. In rural Grenada, a mother may exhort her daughter to "bring a child for me to mind. Mih frock open wide." These are usually women plagued by a feeling of "something missing". Their days may be full with various activities, some of them income-generating on a small scale. Yet such activity may not be totally fulfilling. These are women (and they are all over the Caribbean, not just in Grenada alone) whose society has conditioned them to see themselves as baby-bearers and baby-carers. Their very sense of identity is inextricably tied up in these functions. An emptiness overcomes them once their own babies have matured and left home. Hence their exhortations for "a child to mind". And often, in caring for their children's children, these women come into their own and enjoy their roles of baby-carers even more than the first time around. The difference is, of course, that they are now old hands at the game, plus the fact that they are no longer plagued by the general problems that went with managing their own families. Those general problems are now someone else's concern, not theirs.

In Trinidad and Guyana, where the descendants of the original Hindu East Indian immigrants comprise a significant portion of the population, a corresponding pattern of support exists. But, unlike the system which obtains in the wider Caribbean, this one has its basis in formalized family rituals dating back to early India. Up until even the 1960s, the predominant custom dictated that the newly wed Hindu couple would take up residence within the household of the bridegroom's family. Today, however, as the agents of change sweep through the Caribbean, even this well entrenched custom is disappearing. Importantly, though, the mechanisms and benefits attendant upon this custom can still be found within Hindu families.

Traditionally, when the "dulahen" or new bride entered her mother-in-law's home, it became the mother-in-law's function to integrate this new and most subordinate member into her new family. She passed on to her daughter-in-law lessons in housewifery and household management. She also served as a mediator between the young couple, helping them to adjust to each other and to stabilize their relationship. The young bride spent the first two weeks of her marriage, even before its consummation, back with her own family. During this transition period, again in woman to woman support, her mother would prepare her for the entry into her husband's household. Later, after a year of marriage, she would again visit her mother's household for another ritualized breather away from her marital home.

In all of this, the children of the unions enjoyed the attention and care of female relatives from both sides of the family tree. The modern Hindu couple in the Caribbean may or may not follow the customary forms. But for them, the essence of the traditional patterns continue to enrich the families. The benefits are theirs for the taking. And that is nowhere more prevalent than in the area of child-care. In just about every family, there is an older female relative who cares for the children.

But what about the children who are the objects of all this care? What impact does it have on them? I had occasion to observe my seven-year-old son and my mother interacting with each other during a vacation period. There they were making kites, hammering away, agreeing, disagreeing, laughing and quarrelling. Out of it came a deeper bond, not just between grandmother and grandson, but between generations. In such mutual sharing, our young and old find opportunities to understand each other better and to establish meaningful communication lines. More than this, life skills, family history, cultural traditions and the like wend their way through the generations. For this same reason, in the past, we Caribbean women had no need of a "Dr Spock" to guide us in child-care. We learned directly from our mothers and other female relatives.

Today the pattern is changing. Dr Spock is appearing in our bookstores. This is a corollary of development. As we women, along with our nations, make and grasp the opportunities that lead to self-actualization, our familiar patterns will, of necessity, change. Even now, there are already some grandmothers enjoying fulfilling careers, looking forward to being able to travel and relax when they retire. These women are generally not satisfied with "staying home and minding baby"—and are already saying so in no uncertain terms. They enjoy their grandchildren but express this enjoyment in a fashion which allows them to pursue their own interests. Hence the growing need for day-care centres in some of our larger islands and capital cities. And when this present generation retires, the situation will be even more pronounced.

This observation is not intended to cause panic. Rather it is made with the intention that we realize the importance of beginning today to build into our communities the support systems which would fulfil the multiplicity of functions which are met by the woman-to-woman extended family support now in existence.

Part 4: Women and Education

Chapter 14: Education and Women's Place in Caribbean Society

by Pat Ellis

The territories of the English speaking Caribbean have all inherited a common legacy from their colonizers in the form of an education system which has had, and continues to have, far-reaching repercussions on the lives of Caribbean people. It is only within very recent times, however, that attention has begun to be focused on the effects that this education has had on the lives of Caribbean women and that attempts are being made to understand how the education to which they have been exposed has determined the place that they occupy within the society. Women are taught their "place" through socialization at home and at school and education has been a major factor in defining their status and the roles that they play in Caribbean society.

It is important to place the education of Caribbean women and the effects that education has had on them within the wider historical framework and socio-economic context of the development of the region since the days of slavery. Inevitably their place has emerged from and been determined by the modes of economic production and the social relationships which existed in the plantation system introduced by the British colonizers. This cultural domination by the colonial rulers was enforced and reinforced by the legal, political, religious and educational institutions which they transplanted into the colonial societies in the region. Through these institutions the small white upper-class elite were able to successfully impose their cultural hegemony and rule and control the large black population.

The education system introduced into the colonies was based on that of nineteenth-century Victorian England. It alienated the local people from their environment, denigrated local culture, traditional values and norms; and because it was educating people to serve a developing British capitalist society, it bore little relevance to the situation, needs or problems of the local West Indian population. Inevitably the sexism and sex stereotypes which were a part of the British system were transmitted to the Caribbean. The image of the male as the head of the household and as the breadwinner with economic responsibility for the family, of the "ideal woman" as housewife and mother, frail and feminine, helpless and genteel were values of a British middle class which ignored the plight of working-class women in Britain, they were nonetheless thought right and proper for the colonial societies of the Caribbean.

As organized education expanded, boys and girls of the lower classes were educated in the same school; but the stereotypes were being firmly entrenched as the sexes pursued separate activities. While the boys were trained to be skilled artisans, the girls were trained to be domestic servants; and this primary education was seen as sufficient for children of this class.

Secondary education for boys and girls of the upper and middle classes— white and coloured/mulatto—was provided in single sexed first-grade and second-grade grammar schools respectively. Here there were clear divisions and distinctions based on colour, class and sex and reinforced by the curriculum. Upper-class white boys were trained for the professions and for senior posts in the colonial administration, middle-class boys received a 'second-grade' education which prepared them for commercial life and for the civil service, while middle- and upper-class girls were being trained to be good mothers, wives and companions worthy of educated husbands. It is significant to note that although upper- and middle-class girls had access to higher education both the content—needlework and domestic subjects—and the purpose of their education was similar to that of their black sisters in the lower class.

Education and the Move Towards National Identity and Independence

The 20th century saw a rapid expansion of the colonial education system and more children from the lower classes gained access to primary as well as to secondary education. Consequently education became an avenue for social mobility and for achieving higher economic and social status within the society. In the 1930s and 1940s a black educated professional middle class began to emerge, a large majority of whom were from lower-class backgrounds. Among this group of Caribbean males a significant number had received higher university education in Britain. Eventually they began to display a growing awareness and a "Caribbean consciousness" and it was they who initiated the move towards self-government in the 1950s and eventual national independence in the 1960s and the 1970s.

This shift in consciousness prompted the desire to move from a situation of total dependence on colonial values and led to the realization of the need to develop a sense of Caribbean national identity and to build independent nation states. By the middle of the century it was being widely accepted that education was not only the key to social mobility but also to national development. At the same time the concept of equal opportunity and access to education for all children of all races and classes introduced an ideology of equality through universal education.

But in reality the economic and social inequalities still existed because of the unequal distribution of wealth in the society. This resulted in significant differences in the choices that were available to boys and girls of different classes both in terms of education and of employment. Nonetheless the new ideology based on the concepts of equality and nationalism has had far reaching influence on the education system. A number of serious attempts have been made to "Caribbeanize" the school curriculum, to make it more relevant and appropriate to local needs and to ensure that it began to reflect the social reality, cultural values and ideas of Caribbean people.

These initiatives have had concrete results in the form of the establishment of a regional university—the University of the West Indies—in 1948; the establishment of a regional Examinations Council—the Caribbean Examinations Council—in 1976—to replace the Cambridge GCE "O" and "A" level examinations; and the Primary Education Project 1980 within which the curriculum for use in schools in the region is being rewritten. Some of the discrepancies between the culture of the school and that of the home, between that of the text books and that of the wider society, have consequently been removed. Through education, concerted efforts are being made to help Caribbean children and adults to understand and deal with the contradictions and the complexities of their societies as well as with the rapid social and economic changes which are necessary and inevitable in the process of national and regional development.

Women's Participation in Education

When public education was introduced into the West Indian colonies much of it was initially provided by the churces and from the beginning some of the missionary churches—notably the Methodist, the Moravian and the Baptists—attempted to address the needs of lower-class women. The education which they provided was aimed to rescue these poor women from their immoral environment and to teach them to be more "respectable", to be good Christians, good wives and good mothers; in fact to be more like their upper-class sisters and to conform to the norms and values of the dominant culture.

As early as 1840 the Catholic sisters of charity established a school for girls in Dominica. However at both primary and secondary levels girls' education stressed the refining and social graces rather than academic performance. When secondary education became available there were fewer such schools for girls and when boys later received scholarships for secondary schools none were offered to girls. At the tertiary level, too, the only scholarships available at that time were to Oxford and therefore only for boys.

Furthermore the state at this time did not allocate money for girls' education at the secondary level and this limited access to those girls whose parents could afford to pay the fees at private schools run by the churches. This meant that black and coloured girls were automatically excluded. However in some of the smaller islands the state did contribute some funds to the single girls' secondary school which existed, but in all cases the amount was less than that allocated to the secondary school(s) for boys.

With the expansion of education in the 20th Century girls began to participate in larger numbers and by 1960-70 had increased significantly at all

93

levels of the education system. Following the introduction of free secondary education in Trinidad and Tobago, total female attendance (78.4%) at secondary level surpassed that of males (77.7%) and female attendance rates at all levels of the primary/secondary system moved from 75.8% in 1960 to 77.7% in 1970. This reversal of the trend of the late 19th Century was evident in other islands in the region as well. There is also evidence that female performance at GCE "O" Level exams improved relative to that of males and in 1971; 52.93% of all GCE passes at "O" Level were females (Trinidad figures).

Although the participation rates and examination performance of girls at secondary school are high, there is, however, a considerable drop out rate at the tertiary level. One of the factors responsible for this is the high incidence of teenage pregnancies which not only interrupt but more often than not put a premature end to girls' education. Teenage pregnancies in Jamaica accounted for 26% of all births in 1973, 30% in 1974 and 37% in 1975. Since girls who become pregnant are automatically expected to leave school, this often prevents them from taking advantage of the opportunities available for higher education. The sexual stereotyping which has existed in school curricula and text books, the options and choices which girls have been encouraged or forced to make, the attitudes and expectation of their teachers and of the wider society, their perceptions of themselves; all of these contribute to their lower levels of participation at the tertiary levels and to the areas of study in which they find themselves at the university. At the university, therefore, although the level of female participation has increased from 34.6% in 1971 to 41.3% in 1976 and to 43.9% in 1978 (figures for St Augustine Campus, Trinidad only), they still cluster in the faculties of arts and education—the traditional women's subject areas, as the following figures for 1978 (Trinidad Campus) show:

Table 14.1
Girls at University in Trinidad, as a percentage of total

Arts and General Studies	66.4
Agriculture	24.1
Engineering	3.8
Natural Sciences	47.8
Social Sciences	38.5
All Faculties	43.9

Within the education system in the region, there are generally speaking more women than men. The majority of teachers are women and there are more trained female teachers than male; yet fewer positions of seniority and power in the teaching profession and in the education system are held by women than by men. Promotion of women is not as rapid as that of men and there are fewer female head teachers and principals particularly at the secondary and tertiary levels even though the opposite is true at the primary levels, especially in the smaller islands. Management and administration of education is usually concentrated in male hands, but increasingly this is changing and in recent times more women are to be found in such positions. Barbados, Grenada (up to October 1983), Guyana (1970s) and St Lucia have all had female ministers of education while in many of the islands women hold senior positions in ministries of education.

Education, Mobility and Status

Upper- and middle-class women in the Caribbean during the colonial period were part of the small white elite, and, as has already been pointed out, their values and self-image reflected those of the dominant British culture. They were educated for, and acted out, the ideal stereotype roles of wife, mother and companion to a husband who provided for them and on whom they were dependent.

The situation of their black sisters in the lower echelons of the society was drastically different. With access to formal education, girls from this lower-class background, in which it was 'normal and natural' to engage in economic activity, were able to acquire skills and qualifications with which they could command higher paying jobs in the teaching, nursing and civil service. This not only increased their economic and social status, but it injected into the "newly educated middle class" aspects of a value system which was different from the ideology of the stereotyped image of the ideal woman which an earlier middle class had sought to perpetuate.

Both women and men of the new professional middle class were expected to conform to the norms and to emulate the dominant culture of the upper class. Moreover the test of their education was often the degree to which they disassociated themselves from their lower-class—and by implication inferior— culture. Educated women caught in this contradiction aspired and strove to acquire the values of the upper class, but at the same time continued to play important roles in the rural communities from which they had come.

They contributed in no small way to the development of these communities by giving of their services (often free of charge) and skills as nurses, teachers, leaders and organizers of community groups. They served as role models and motivated others to improve their situation through education. They continued to be the main economic support for their families and were generally held in high regard and esteem by members of their communities; and they continue to be leading figures in the life and affairs of many communities in the region even today.

But because the education system continues to reflect an ideology of which sexism is an integral part, many educated middle-class women have internalized the ideal image of a woman as wife and mother dependent on a male. The distance between this official ideal stereotype and the actual behaviour of these women is manifested by the double standards in Caribbean society, where married women expect and are expected by their husbands to contribute substantially to the financial support of their families, while at the same time society sees them as inferior to and dependent on their husbands. Their economic independence has not in fact guaranteed them real independence.

At another level, although women from the lower class operate by and large outside of the official stereotype—which is in conflict with their reality— they have still internalized its models as right; and their self-image and self-worth are affected by this. They socialize their children to aspire through education to "middle-classness" and to the stereotyped roles which society expects them to play as adults. This perpetuates the conflict between the ideal and the actual roles that women play and even though girls are socialized to be wives and mothers, their socialization also equips them with strategies that will ensure their economic survival independently of the male.

There can be no doubt that as a result of education many Caribbean women have been able to attain high levels of achievement and to hold positions of influence and responsibility both in the public and private sector. Women are lawyers, journalists, engineers, managers, doctors, permanent secretaries in government ministries and directors. More recently in the last decade women have made a breakthrough into occupational areas which had previously been dominated by men. Women are now employed as mechanics, welders, agronomists, bus drivers, ministers of government and ministers of religion, and the lone female prime minister. And though women are still not visible in large numbers in the highest levels of decision-making in politics this breakthrough by the few and the steady increase in their numbers are important steps towards ensuring that the female part of the Caribbean population is adequately represented in all spheres and at all levels of Caribbean society.

Women, Education and Change in Caribbean Society

Control by the dominant culture is never total; the dominated group continues to have its own counter-culture rooted in its own experiences and social reality. The contradiction between the dominant British culture and the social reality of Caribbean people, and the tension and conflict which this generated, has led the latter to seek to redefine, to reform and replace the former by a Caribbean culture which incorporates aspects of the plurality of cultures that exist in these islands.

The present stated development goals of the various territories contrast and conflict sharply with the previous development patterns of the colonial era; there has been general agreement that the transformation of their economic structures and a redefinition of social relationships are essential. Within this context the need to address the roles and relationships which existed between men and women is of key importance.

The Formal Education System

As Caribbean people strive to come to terms with their history, with the contradictions and complexities of their social reality, they have continued to see education and the school as vehicles through which the boys and girls, men and women can be mentally and psychologically prepared to fight the various types of oppression—including sexual oppression—which exist in their societies. Recognizing that attitudes and perceptions of male-female roles are inculcated and reinforced in schools, a number of initiatives have been taken to address the existing stereotyping within the curriculum and to sensitize teachers and students alike to this issue. Sessions have been held with teachers in various training colleges, in primary and secondary schools and with subject teachers who are involved in rewriting and developing new curricula and teaching materials for use in primary and secondary schools in the region. Similar sessions have been held with guidance teachers and with students— male and female—to make them more aware of the need for students to be exposed to wider subject options and career choices.

Supplementary reading material and modules on women have also been introduced in a few schools and sensitizing sessions have been conducted within several university courses. All these have formed the basis for a slowly expanding women's studies programme on the three campuses of the UWI. On each campus, Cave Hill in Barbados, Mona in Jamaica and St Augustine in Trinidad, there is a women's studies group with a coordinator. These groups have been meeting regularly and have organized a number of seminars and discussions at which papers on various aspects of the lives of women have been presented. There are plans to compile from these papers a reader which could be used as a text book in a women's studies course. At the same time, by participating in the activities of these groups, lectures and tutors are being sensitized and some are introducing a women's component/perspective into their respective courses.

Gradually a body of knowledge about women along with relevant curriculum materials is being built up and becoming available for use in educational institutions in the region. As the curriculum is being rewritten systematic attempts are being made to remove the sex bias in text books and teaching material. Special units on women have been introduced into social science, history, literature and other subject areas. Supplementary reading material on the lives, situation, roles and needs of Caribbean women is being prepared and made available to schools and the educational institutions. Special sensitizing sessions on the role and status of women are being conducted in seminars and workshops, in primary and secondary schools and in teacher training colleges as well as within various faculties of the UWI. Within the university, the Institute of Social and Economic Research (ISER) and the Woman and Development Unit (WAND) of the Extra-Mural Department have been responsible for promoting and conducting research on the lives of Caribbean women. This has greatly expanded the data base and provided pertinent information about women at all levels of the society. They have been responsible for producing a continuous amount of documentation, communications and resource materials which are being circulated in the region. In particular WAND has developed a documentation and resource centre through which it packages this information for different groups using a wide range of media including newsletters, occasional papers, booklets, posters, audio tapes, slide tapes, video tapes. Work is also being done at the Regional Pre-School Child Development Centre (RPCDC) at UWI, Jamaica, on child-rearing practices and the socialization process in order to encourage parents and teachers of young children to adopt a non-sexist approach and to be more conscious of how their attitudes affect the children's development.

All of the above initiatives are taking place simultaneously and will therefore have a ripple-multiplier effect. The information on and about the experiences of women is being fed into the formal education system at all levels. The hope is that it will also be used to provide guidelines for coherent social policies which recognize not only the needs and concerns of Caribbean women, but which draws on their skills and talents to implement them.

Adult Non-formal Education Programmes (NFE)

Outside of the formal education system, black lower-class women in the Caribbean have been involved in NFE programmes since the days of slavery. Initially they participated in such programmes as were organized by the churches and various welfare groups. Later in the 1930s and 1940s they participated in trade union activities and in women's voluntary movements; in the programmes of community development and social welfare agencies.

Middle-class women were also involved in voluntary organizations such as the Red Cross, the YWCA, Church groups and Women's Federations. They usually saw themselves as providing a service for their less fortunate sisters in the poorer communities, and their groups as playing a social rather than an educational role. They focused on social welfare, leisure time and cultural activities, but nevertheless they did have an educational impact, for they transmitted the ideas, values and norms of the middle class which they represented. In addition they passed on a variety of traditional gender-specific skills in child-care, nutrition and home economics. In this way the official stereotype image of women was reinforced, and the belief that their main aspiration in life ought to be that of being competent wives and mothers, was perpetrated.

Today there are large number of these Non-Governmental Organizations (NGOs) in every island in the region—ranging from 13 in Antigua to 43 in St Lucia. They operate on a voluntary basis, and organize and run a variety of programmes and projects in which hundreds of women are involved. Although many of these programmes are short-term and ad hoc and only offer the traditional female activities many women have gained valuable experience and skills in leadership, planning, organization and management through their involvement in such programmes. In the light of this, these organizations and their community groups are increasingly being seen as vehicles for harnessing and developing the potential of women and for bringing about positive changes in their lives. From its inception, the university too has been involved in providing adult education in which many women from all levels of the society have participated. Through its Extra-Mural Department in the university centres in the various islands it has played an important role in providing opportunities for women to be exposed to a wide range of subjects including academic, non-academic, vocational and non-vocational. Women have benefited from programmes such as public health, public administration, social work, pre-school education, Caribbean drama, dance, music, among others; they also participate actively in seminars, workshops and lectures which aim to stimulate public opinion and a broad-based programme of citizenship education. Women are not involved in these programmes only as participants, for a significant number of the course tutors, specialist and resident tutors have been, and continue to be, women.

Caribbean leaders like their counterparts in other developing countries have come to realize that the disadvantages which they have suffered and inherited as ex-colonial people cannot be cured by reliance on education only within the formal system, but that there is need to tackle them simultaneously through adult non-formal education programmes. There is a growing awareness of the potential which these programmes have for building awareness, upgrading skills, motivating personal growth and generally facilitating the process of national development. Many governments in the region have recently formulated national plans for adult education. But few if any of these plans have paid any serious attention to addressing the changing roles and relationships of men and women in contemporary Caribbean society and many of them still reflect a sex bias towards the traditional 'female' content and the stereotypes that embody the underlying ideology of patriarchy and male dominance.

Some of the NGOs engaged in NFE have, however, begun to show more sensitivity to the issues concerning women and their place in Caribbean society. The Caribbean Council of Churches in their education for development programme, service clubs, the YWCA, the Caribbean Women's Association, the trade unions and other voluntary organizations have all begun in their community programmes to focus on the role and situation of women. Within these programmes women have the opportunity to upgrade their skills in family life and education, in small business management, and project development. In many programmes too there is more emphasis on self-development and awareness building and their more diversified content is exposing women at the community level to knowledge and skills which is not only broadening their horizons but increasing their employment options. In addition these agencies and organizations have been instrumental in building and strengthening a network among Caribbean women and in so doing are contributing to the growing sense of common purpose and solidarity.

The UWI has and is playing a crucial role in the drive to raise the consciousness of all Caribbean people about the issues, needs and concerns of women and about their role and status within the society. This is being done mainly through its Women and Development Unit (WAND) which was established in 1978. The Unit's programme is really a broad-based integrated non-formal education programme which focuses on women in rural communities in the region. The Unit is therefore fulfilling one of the key functions of the adult education programme of the university which had been identified as early as 1945 by the late Dr Eric Williams who saw even then that:

> In its adult education programme the U.W.I. must have a special role to play in the education of women, who still are so heavily handicapped by their economic status and by the traditional conception of their role in society. The U.W.I. should struggle in theory and in practice to give women that equality in the social order which will enable them to make the contribution to their community which they should but do not now make.

Conclusion

It is extremely difficult for women to break with traditions, to challenge the customs and to dispel the myths about their place in their societies. By and large the education that Caribbean women have received has not equipped them for such a task. The nature of this education is now being widely questioned. There is a realization that if education is to have any *real* value for women it must not only raise their consciousness about the oppressive structures that keep them in positions of powerlessness, but also help them to understand the nature of the social, economic and political systems in which they operate and which operate against them. In order to achieve this there is a need for both formal education institutions and informal and non-formal education organizations which can develop and implement programmes that will reorient the purpose of education towards ensuring that it prepares all Caribbean people, women and men, to participate fully and equally in the process of development of the region. To change the negative images that society has of women and that many women have of themselves is a challenge to Caribbean women no less than to Caribbean men.

Chapter 15: Vocational Education for Girls in Trinidad and Tobago in the early 20th Century

by Angela Hamel-Smith

Before the Second World War, girls and women within both the education system and the broader society, laboured under certain disadvantages. The small privileged group of girls, usually middle-class, who enjoyed a secondary education, were exposed to a limited curriculum and, therefore, effectively restricted from competing for university scholarships. All of this was due to the assumption of the era that the only career open to respectable women was marriage and if respectable women wanted to or were forced to support themselves, nothing was wrong with their having to endure lower rates of pay. While the average black or coloured working class girl had the same access to primary education as her brother, she had little or no access to vocational training or secondary education. When she did become a member of the work force, it was usually in an unskilled occupation and her earnings were less than those of men performing the same task.

However, the position of women in Trinidad was not very different from their position in other countries; in fact, in certain respects it was probably more favourable. Indeed by 1940 there were grounds for certain optimism. Literacy rates for black and coloured men and women were similar, and even for the traditionally restricted East Indian women the situation was brightening. The census of 1946 referred to the fact that while among the older generation of women (over 45 years) the illiteracy rate was 90%, among the 10-14 year age group the illiteracy rate had been "brought down" to 24%. This indicated that by the early 1940s, Indian girls were attending school in greater numbers. By the 1930s, the number and proportion of girls attending secondary schools was steadily increasing and girls in Trinidad could, and did, sit and win college exhibitions with creditable frequency. Considering that Trinidad was a small island with a colonial government the women in the colony did make notable strides between 1900 and 1938. Further gains had to await the post-war period when political developments would propel many women to join the popular agitation for political independence and universal suffrage alongside their husbands and brothers.

Up to 1938, there was no provision for training girls in any vocation or trade if we exclude essentially domestic skills; indeed, the idea of imparting technical skills to girls was virtually non-existent. Most girls were taught sewing in primary school and the large number of seamstresses reported in the census returns bore witness to the fact that many women earned or supplemented their income in this way. There is no record of girls being apprentices, and the general assumption was that only boys were eligible for apprenticeship.

It was not until 1938 that any specific call for vocational training for girls was heard. In that year, the Special Committee on Vocational Education considered the question of domestic service training which they saw as an analogy to the apprenticeship system for boys. The Committee observed that, despite a demand for household labour, most nursemaids, cooks and butlers entered domestic service with no preparatory training for such work. The census returns for the period indicate that this was an occupational area in which women had always predominated. In 1901, women constituted 86% of the 23,259 personal service workers in the colony, and up to 1938 they always accounted for 80-90% of this group. However, while the proportion of women in the group remained constant, the numbers involved declined after 1921. This indicates that fewer women were seeking domestic employment and this would have given rise to increased complaints by middle- and upper-class persons about the difficulty of finding efficient domestic workers. This pattern is consistent with the complaints of the Special Committee that the "better type" girl refused to enter domestic service. Clearly the more ambitious and energetic girls were seeking alternatives.

The Special Committee felt that a new and thorough system of domestic service training would both produce a more efficient worker, and attract the "better type" of girl. The Committee complained that it was difficult to attract girls who had successfully completed seventh standard to enter domestic work. The girls who did enter household employment were those who left primary school at an earlier age with but a smattering of knowledge. In an attempt to uplift the standards and status of this occupation, both a part-time and full-time course were recommended. The content was to include correct cooking, the nutritional value of food and housewifery.

The Special Committee also observed that if domestic service was made "more attractive by employers" then a better quality of girl would be recruited. However, they made no recommendation about suitable wages, not even for the future graduates of the proposed training course. The existing wages were very low. In the early 1920s, a female butler started at $5.00 per month, while a male butler began at $10.00, exactly twice as much. Similarly, a female cook usually earned from $6.00-12.00 per month, while a male groom was paid between $10.00 and $24.00 per month. These jobs usually provided accommodation. The fact that the majority of persons in this occupational group were women meant that the lowest wages were the norm.

This was a problem in all islands, and in 1939 the West India Royal Commission made some sympathetic and revealing comments on the position of women employed as domestic servants. They said that the normal working day for the domestic servant was from 6 a.m. to 9 p.m.—a 15-hour day. And any sick leave, annual holiday or other time of release from duty depended on the "good will" of her employer. Wages were very low and varied between $6.00 and $12.00 a month; after paying rent for the room and buying food virtually nothing was left over.

The Commissioners also observed that, in the West Indies, a large number of women were employed in agriculture at very low wages. It should be pointed out that, despite this, girls were never included in agriculture classes. Women were employed in a variety of tasks requiring heavy physical labour, like unloading coal and sand barges, carrying stones on the road, and bananas on the docks. Generally, the level of pay for women was even lower than men, and many women often received less than a living wage. The Commissioners went on to observe that the problem of low wages was worsened by the fact that in the West Indies, because of promiscuity and illegitimacy, the woman was "so often...the supporter of the home". The traditional justification for offering women lower wages was that they were not the main breadwinner of the family. While this assumption was incorrect in the West Indies, it continued to be applied, resulting in a stressful and depressing situation for many working-class women.

Chapter 16: Women's Participation in Non-Formal Education Activities

by Beryl Carasco

Percentages may differ slightly and the programme orientation shift somewhat; but from Jamaica in the north to Trinidad in the south the trends are markedly similiar. The Non-Formal Education (NFE) activities in which women engage are very visible in the Caribbean region. Indeed, all of the islands can boast of the establishment of organizations, programmes and projects addressing the NFE needs of the female population.

While the indication is that low-income, rural women in the 30-50 age range have increasing access to NFE programmes—many of which are exclusively geared to these women—it is also clear that women's inability to attend regularly and complete these programmes is simultaneously increasing. The reasons are not novel ones and range from lack of motivation and conflict with domestic work to adverse female and male attitudes towards women's participation and the inaccessibility of certain NFE activities on account of location.

At national levels, organizations involved in the NFE of women span a broad spectrum of the society and include governmental, social, religious, political, trade union, youth and professional groups. The non-formal education of women consequently encompasses several areas of activity, including a high concentration of community self-help projects, agricultural extension programmes and craft centres. Only a negligible number of women's programmes which started off as small income-generating or training projects have grown into well established centres, employing full-time staff and producing items for sale. The majority (an overwhelming 90%) of programmes for women continue to be operated on a short-term basis (workshops and seminars) and tend to be deficient in the essentials of post-training, follow-up, stability and viability which programme continuity normally provides.

Several programmes incorporate one or the other of the crucial areas of skills transfer and income-generation with self development, family life guidance and health education components. The low priority given, therefore, to these basic personal enrichment and awareness-raising aspects of women's educational and developmental needs suggests that women (or perhaps those who develop NFE activities for them) may be abandoning these aspects of the programmes for the more lucrative income-generating, skills-oriented ones.

Yet ironically, 75% of the NFE skills training programmes focus on the transfer of handicraft, domestic, and related—largely traditional—skills, which are undoubtedly intended to keep women in marginal modes of employment; while 90% of income-generating projects for women suffer on account of tenuous marketing outlets and economic exploitation of female labour. In Jamaica, Grenada and Montserrat, however, women's NFE programmes generally reflect increased training in non-traditional areas such as construction, cooperatives and scientific agriculture in Jamaica; woodwork, civic awareness and literacy in Grenada; and management skills, industrial related skills and desirable work attitudes in Montserrat. Integrated NFE projects which effectively combine skills training, personal development and income-generation elements are virtually non-existent—except in the cases of isolated projects in St Vincent, Jamaica and Trinidad. In Jamaica, for instance, women are integrated into large development projects as well as into smaller continuing education programmes.

Quite apart from being greatly involved in NFE activities as participants, women are included as project tutors and field level practitioners; but they are not incorporated to any satisfactory extent as programme planners, supervisors, researchers, consultants, evaluators and decision-makers. The challenge, then, to the women of the region is that of raising their level of consciousness in developmental issues, while equipping themselves with the skills which will make them dynamically involved in the growth of the society and the maintenance of their families. NFE must of necessity address itself to the question of how women are going to fit into and contribute to the future of their communities and countries. As such, women's projects and programmes will have to assume wider dimensions and relate more explicitly to larger national, regional and international issues in order to ensure that women are an integral part of the total process of development.

Part 5: Women and Culture

Chapter 17: The Role of Women in Caribbean Culture

by Cheryl Williams

All women play critical roles in culture. As child nurturers and teachers they transmit the values of the society. Their role varies according to the values, institutions and structures of power in that society. Their culture varies according to race and class, rural or urban settlement and over space and time. Some see the Caribbean woman as playing a formative role in the culture; others see her as merely supportive of the general trends.

All Caribbean peoples are products of several dynamic cultural processes which began in slavery and are still continuing. We are all Creoles sharing a complex heritage but relating to it differently if we are African, Indian or European. Each of us at varying levels has retained some of our ancestral norms, adopted new values from other races; and the inevitable mixing has led to the emergence of syncretic or Creole values.

Euro-Creole Women

In this complexity the story of the Euro-Creole woman is simplest. From slavery to the present the general drive of these societies has been towards the acquisition of European values. The prevailing assumptions about the superiority of European culture caused both the European man and woman to attempt to recreate in the Caribbean the culture of their mother country. For most people that culture would remain the desired standard. The women here were not cultural creators but saw themselves as defenders of the inherited values. From the beginning, however, they were shaped by their new environment. They adopted many aspects of the slaves' culture in dress, food and speech. In the end visitors recognized them for what they were, Euro-Creoles. They were no longer Europeans living in the tropics but Creoles with an altered sensibility. This created a conflict within them which pervades the literature. Many attempt to come to terms with their Creoleness, while others recoil and, although they increasingly share the Creole world, the problem of identity remains a real one for them.

Black Women

On the other hand from the beginning black women played a most formidable cultural role. The similarity of culture among the various tribes led to the existence of a single African world view. Plantation society destroyed many of the material and institutional aspects of this African culture such as the political and economic institutions—the very ones dominated by men. Those areas of culture which were most important to the Africans and which did not come into serious conflict with the plantation survived best. These were generally the intimate areas, those dominated by the women, and included religion, song, dance, folklore, an African pharmacopeia and healing and architecture. From the beginning the women were the most important bearers of the traditions, a role increased by the prevalence of matriarchal homes. Men did take leading roles though many of their activities were banned or harassed by the authorities. In Maroon communities men were better placed to carry on their traditional roles. Much of what was allowed to survive was marginal and therefore vulnerable, but also enabled people to live comfortably with various traditions. Hence acculturation to European values did paradoxically take place in the very areas, such as religion, where ancestral values persisted most; and out of the mix of the African and European was born the Creole culture. It is here that black women were most active. There is no doubt that they were a driving force in the development and sustenance of indigenous relations such as the Shango, Santeria, Kumina and Spiritual Baptist. Blacks also adopted European forms such as Christianity and Africanized them. Conversely African forms grew more Europeanized; but in times of distress, and there were many, culture became more African. In post-emancipation Jamaica the Christian Baptists moved nearer to the more Africanized Native Baptist and in Trinidad the French Bele dance became more of an ancestral spirit dance. In "better" economic times, there was a greater adoption of European norms. Culture, the only area over which blacks retained some control, was the centre of both creativity and revolt. Combine the woman's cultural role with her roles as peasant, labourer, trader, urban domestic and usually the head of a matriarchal home and we understand why she is so often portrayed as the strong, survivalist Caribbean woman.

Much of this creativity happened in the post-emancipation period. For the black and the poor the existing race and class divisions encouraged cultural duality, whether they were part of the powerful black peasantries which were then established or part of the large service sectors of the towns. In the larger society the white bias continued. For Europeans the belief in the superiority of British culture grew stronger.

After the 1900s

After the 1900s the black woman's predominant cultural role was to alter. The decline of the peasantry, urbanization, some industrialization, the new emphasis on anglicization, the introduction of education and the fact that social mobility was defined in European terms meant a growth in the Europeanization of these societies. In the process of anglicization the role of women diminished in Trinidad, for instance, the decline of the patois meant the death of much of the folklore—the proverbs [that moralizing education of most of our mothers], some Yoruba dances and ceremonies of initiation, birth, death and fertility. The "women's culture" became even more of an alternative, known but marginal, alive but less respected.

There were new interesting movements in the culture which seemed to give men a more powerful role. The duality of culture was never more evident than from the 1920s. From entertainment to religion more European forms were adopted. Cricket became popular and in many of these European imports men took leadership roles—as was customary in Europe. Some of these forms which seemed outwardly European had African elements. These included the penny banks, burial societies, lodges, agricultural societies and labour unions. But even while Europeanization increased, cultural creativity continued amongst the poor. Most interestingly, the new Creole forms were more urban-based, in contrast to the rural base of the women's culture, they were male creations, male centred and dominated by men. Calypso and steelband are the best examples of these; calypso contains a very heavy anti-feminine streak.

East Indian Women

The role of East Indian women is paradoxical. Theoretically, she is seen as divine—a reflection of the goddess Laskhmi—the feminine complement of the man. In practice, her culture is male-dominated. The man takes the lead in religion, the family, economy, politics and the public sphere. The imbalance in numbers among the early East Indian immigrants gave the early woman a greater freedom and independence. But during indentureship some attempts were made to balance the proportions of male and female and on the plantations it was possible to recreate some family life and culture—unlike the African experience. The later establishment of Indian villages and peasantries allowed for a greater re-creation of the culture. Men remained the leaders, the women's role was supportive. Women had known and inherited roles in rituals, songs, religion, funerals and weddings. They sustained much, although there were no great departures as in the case of black women. To some they still had much cultural power. To others, such as Vidia and Seepersad Naipaul their role was clichéd and limited and they were exploited by men who imperfectly practised the tradition. But Indian culture had to adapt to the new circumstances and there was indeed Indo-Creolization, internal changes to the culture as well as those prompted by external forces. Some rituals were changed and some choice was allowed in marriages. Conversion to Presbyterianism and its schools hastened some westernization—but only among a few. The late entry of Indians into the wider education system in the 1940s, the identification with India, the building of Hindu schools and temples, all encouraged the persistence of traditional values.

After the 1940s

The 1940s and after were times of critical role and culture changes for everyone. Education, the desire for mobility, politics, increasing urbanization and modernization and the growing impact of the media and American culture increased the European bias in these societies still further. Moreover the decline of the black peasantries and the crisis of poverty further undermined the value placed on the worlds which contained the folk culture.

It is in Caribbean literature that the most powerful role for women emerges, whether consciously or subconsciously. All, especially the women, girded themselves for change. In a harsh milieu those peasant or urban women, willing to do anything they could to earn a living, were seen as a tower of strength in the Caribbean world. Embattled though they were, they were ever stoical, they were the survivors. Only in the literature about whites are the women presented as delicate and dependent in contrast with the sensuality of the coloured woman, while the men are often portrayed as weak, emasculated types compensating for the bludgeoning of the system by a superficial machismo.

Both the African and Indian women had dreams that revealed the complexity of their lives. They all dreamt of education and social mobility, and these dreams were focused on their sons who became what Edward Kamau Braithwaite calls their '*lux occidente*' or western lights. The son's progress would be that of the race. But the literature records that as the men became more mobile they became Saxonized and there was a clash in sensibility between the men and the women. The men seemed more imprisoned by cultural ambivalence; the women, poorer, and therefore closer to the Creole world, seemed on firmer cultural soil. The cultural revolt, spontaneous and subliminal, the centre of women's power, was being subsumed to the political revolt. And it was the men who led the political revolt be it in the labour, or nationalist, or intellectual movements. The rise of nationalism did bring some pride in the old forms and some revivalism. Some governments gave lip-service to the idea of a national culture and some of the song and dance aspects of the culture are celebrated. But even here the real folk culture dies. The Bele is no longer ancestral ritual, but stylized dance. Much of the folk culture remains, but substantive portions are simply nostalgia. The contemporary urban Creole world is more syncretic, Europeanized, and male-centred, because for the sons who became leaders the central concerns were political and economic. Too often culture was disregarded. Indeed, the idea of progress and development is based on the urban industrial models of Europe, further increasing the Europeanization of these societies.

Yet the pendulum shifts continually between acculturation, revivalism and creativity. New cultures emerged, but these too had a male bias. Jamaican Rastafarianism, the Black Power and Black Muslim movements sought to overturn Eurocentric dominance. All celebrated the virtues of womanhood and sought to rebuild the black family. But in these movements men are clearly seen as the leaders although the women are expected to nuture the traditions of the group. As the men had joined those creations that women dominated, so women now joined the men's, for example, the calypso and steelband. Moreover the coincidence between class and culture continues, for with increased mobility women's participation in Europeanized cultural activities has likewise increased.

Vidia Naipaul's *A House for Mr Biswas* reflects the two major cultural movements for Indians. Biswas the male seeks education and mobility. He acts, and his woman follows. The powerful Hindu matriarch Mrs Tulsi attempts to preserve the traditions; but as the drives of the larger society increase she too seeks education and urbanization. Yet she still attempts to conserve the traditions. As in the real world there were many cultural changes, including westernization and the downgrading of Creole values. The changes, especially in religion, rituals and the family diminished the women's role. Yet, as in the black world, there were survivals and many of these would re-emerge with the cultural revivalisms of the 1970s. As for the African woman, these revivals had two paradoxical trends. Some of the forms in which Indian women still play a prominent role are Divali, the festival of Kali Mai, the weeping rituals of the Hoosay and at weddings. The revival of the Indian family is also seen as essential. Yet westernization did introduce notions of equality which contradicted the emphasis on the sanctity of womanhood that is often accompanied by male dominance and imprisons rather than liberates women. It is not accidental that arranged marriages are on the rise again. In most areas men continue to lead and women play a supportive role. As with the contemporary African women, many fail to appreciate the tremendous role the East Indian woman plays in most cultural practices. Yet Kumar Mahabir, an Indo-Trinidadian researcher, points out that on the syncretic and intercultural level Indian women seem to lead, whereas men dominate the revivals. Women for instance, are more prone to intermarry; women comprise many of the devotees of that syncretic Trinidadian worship of La Divina Pastora (the black Kalizo); women composed and sang many of the early Indo-Creole songs and are even now major singers in the local Indian song competitions, although so far there have only been male Indian calypsonians. The ancestral and Creole aspects of their culture continue to survive amidst threats.

In conclusion, the signals are paradoxical. Women continue to play an important role in culture but it is now mainly supportive. It is in the traditional cultures that her role was more prominent and as these decline or become more syncretic so does her leadership role decline. Much of the cultural initiative has been taken from her in contemporary times. Neither the family nor the powerless individual can stem the prevailing cultural tides for it is larger, more impersonal forces which dictate cultural values. The social and political institutions, the values of the elites in charge, the education, the technologies, the media and the idea about the good life are what dictate cultural values; and the trend here is still largely Eurocentric. The woman seems largely impotent in this milieu. She too joins those who succumb, or the embattled ones who, following that ancient cultural law, continue to revive, gain and recreate. But at the present time the nature and extent of her power is much imperilled.

Chapter 18: Media Concepts for Human Development in the Caribbean with Special Reference to Women

by Claudette Earl

Social Awareness

The Caribbean woman, like women the world over, is confronted with the battery of complexities that comprise modern life. She is conscious of her new-found economic independence, her religious loyalties (however repressed they might be), the emerging sense of nationalism in the Caribbean, her maternal potential and its concomitant psychological pressures. The Caribbean woman is affected by the world economic crisis; she has to be concerned with the spiralling cost of living and also the issues of child-care, abortions, maternal health standards, vocational training, population movement and unemployment.

But unlike most of her sisters in the metropolitan countries, the Caribbean woman has to understand the politics of development so that she will be able to appreciate moves by regional leaders who are working in the interest of the four-and-a-half million people in the area. No Caribbean person, man or woman, would be naive enough to believe that the external question of the rich and poor nations, as highlighted by the affluent life-styles of the developed countries and the starving humans in Bangladesh, does not concern us. The lyrics, 'The rich get richer and the poor get children', as sung in the film *The Great Gatsby*, put in a nutshell the state of affairs between the rich countries and the poor countries. The rich countries always seem to be able to control population and feed themselves while the poor countries like India and certain African states always have food problems of one sort or another while the population growth spirals.

Women in the region have to realize that, although the problems of womanhood are as fundamental as they are universal, the Caribbean woman has a special challenge. Hers is not simply to be a good wife and mother or to be a good career woman who skilfully combines family life and economic existence. The Caribbean woman, like the Caribbean man, has to meet a multiplicity of challenges in order to realize the potential of the Caribbean people.

Social Contradictions

The sensitive press should be aware of the problems of the under-privileged in the society: of the plight of underpaid domestics, of impoverished and deserted single women, of retarded and crippled children whose parents are poor, of women market-vendors who are working hard to maintain themselves and the children and also to save for a house, of women who have no husbands or men to help them, yet work in remote areas and are plagued by theft of their crops, of women and men who are woefully underpaid and who are afraid of 'throwing a spanner in the works' by bringing their situation to the attention of the authorities.

Yet we see pictures of the country's elite with glasses in hands attending cocktail parties and lavish luncheons and dinners. The regularity with which these pictures are published gives testimony to the fact that the press is pandering to the vocal and visible minority of the society and wilfully ignoring the predicament of the broad masses. And it is against such a backdrop of social contradictions that the responsible media must help women and men in the Caribbean to define and attain a quality of life that is socially, economically and culturally relevant.

Awareness for Action

It is not always true that all invention takes place in the white industrial North. Other places, from another totality of experience, however limited, throw up things which are of universal application. Those who have been conditioned to think that everything outside of London, New York or Paris or Rome cannot be taken seriously find this hard to accept. The irony is that with the control of the mass media in the metropolitan centres, and the power attendant on such control, the very original sources are fed back their own products as if they were invented in those centres. Just as our sugar is fed back to us as prettily wrapped confectionery 'made in England' and our bauxite fed back as motor cars, pots and pans, so is our own reggae fed back to us on a million-dollar label by a King of Reggae who is, believe it or not, an American. Even black power was fed back to us as an American invention though Marcus Garvey, Aime Cesaire and Frantz Fanon (all Caribbean men) have become acknowledged prophets.

People who have been subjected to centuries of colonial rule cannot suddenly shed their psychological shackles. They must go through a transitional period during which they reexamine, analyse and review the cultural, social, religious and economic factors out of which they hope to distil a new way of life. Within the last decade, Caribbean leaders have been urging their people to 'look forward' as opposed to 'looking outward' for relevant concepts of life. Yet there are aspects of our life which have not been fully responsive to the winds of change and which in their present form lack social significance.

Thousands of women and men in the region are yet to appreciate the fact that a woman who comes out of the multi-ethnicity of the Caribbean is immediately at a disadvantage in the Miss World or Miss Universe beauty contests. These contests are judged on what is accepted as beauty in the Caucasian world. Why should a woman of a multi-ethnic background demoralize her personhood by participating in such a show? The contest organizers may no doubt decide every few years or so to place a non-white girl among the first three. But even that show of tokenism is restricted to girls of Caucasian features. The Caribbean media should join with vocal social organizations in clamouring for the region's governments to ban Caribbean women from participating in shows.

The Media and Caribbean Women

Too many of our commercials on the electronic media and advertisements in the print media still reflect ideas of an alien and irrelevant culture. Commercials should not confuse people's priorities but should give them constructive help. Film—the most graphic form of mass communication—has not been given its rightful place in the mass communication development thrust in the society. It is regarded mainly as an entertainment medium and its use as an instrument for mass education has been shamefully overlooked. There are so many moving, exciting and imaginative stories that have come out of the vast literature of the West Indies. Yet so few films of note have originated from the region. *Portia Faces Life, Life Can be Beautiful, Peyton Place* and *The Reverend Matthews* have been hogging the electronic media in these parts for the longest while. And although they have been great sources of entertainment for the thousands of women that live vicariously through the popular characters, we may wonder how much longer they must continue to be so. Regional soap operas have come and gone and they were highly acclaimed because persons identified intimately with the West Indian 'yard' characters who featured in the productions. Since the local productions were successes we can venture to suggest that certain West Indian novels can be scripted, serialized and syndicated throughout the region. This would have the added advantage of making people aware of the works of indigenous writers.

The women's page of newspapers and the women's programmes of the electronic media have come under much fire from the Women's Liberation Movement. Women editors have been accused of keeping their sisters oppressed by feeding them with recipes, beauty and diet regimens, fashion features and generally the type of articles that keep women bound in a cocoon of femininity. If a woman is content with being a housewife who should disturb her quietude with revolutionary talk of women's lib? Similarly, if a woman feels that she wants to leave her children with adequate help and define an existence for herself outside her home, then she must not be made to feel guilty about her actions. I think that there is a place in the media of the future for the women's page and the women's programme providing these programmes reorient their contents to meet the needs of a large cross-section of the population. An intelligent woman's editor would use her recipe corner to promote the use of local dishes. This is a most important factor in a society that is in a transitional culinary period. Women's programmes can also be used to instruct women and men on how to make the best nutritional use of seasonal products. Featuring stories of men and women in areas of self-help, housing and farming is another positive aspect of women's programmes, be they print or electronic. It is not an uncommon occurrence for a woman in Guyana to be working on a self-help project alone or with the help of her children. She might be a domestic worker or a market vendor with no other financial resources, but, through a 'box hand' (a Guyanese way of saving), she can join a self-help group. Women who have successfully shouldered such tasks deserve to be commended. One way of doing this is by featuring stories and pictures of the women. If they are shy and not interested in appearing in the newspapers then their stories could be told on the radio so other women might be encouraged to follow suit.

Conclusion

If human development is to happen in the evolving Caribbean, if human development is to improve the quality of life in the Caribbean, the cultural, historical and economic dimensions of the people must be put in proper perspective. People must understand and be committed to the new socio-economic structure which exploits the natural resources of the region for the benefit of the region. The media can help by being itself committed to the social and economic structures of individual countries and also by being sensitive to the needs and aspirations of the people. Such a media can, without doubt, build a common denominator of experience amongst the people and put them on to the road to human dignity.

Chapter 19: Women in Calypso

by Elma Reyes

Can women, by their entry as performers in the calypso world, help to change the negative image of themselves as portrayed in some of the more popular calypsos of Trinidad and Tobago?

Such change is doubtful if the past and current crop of calypsos are any indication, for these portray Caribbean women as money-crazy, promiscuous, evil schemers. Persons who are critical of this image will recognize that women's rights do not seem to be adaptable as a suitable theme by the exponents of calypso—male or female.

For example, in 1980, only two calypsonians seemed to have considered a theme relevant to women's concerns and one of them was a man. In *Take the Number* the man, Scrunter, highlighted the frightening prevalence of sex crimes against women. He sings of the advice he overheard his neighbour giving her teenage daughter, shaping into a catchy refrain her insistence that the girl 'take the number' of any car she happens to travel in if she misses the school bus.

Scrunter's popular calypso, *Woman on the Bass*, is a tribute to the only woman member of a well-known steelband, and serves to document in song the increasing number of women playing in steelbands, a previously male-dominated cultural medium.

Calypsonian Lady Jane also elected to use calypso to deplore the increase in rape, annoying as she did many male members of her audience by her suggestion that the authorities should:

> Send those rapermen to jail
> Beat them with the birch 'til they wail
> Then send in Calypso Jane
> To throw some cat in dey tail

Although 13 women had been advertised as participants in the tents that year, the majority of them could only manage tuneful ditties with superficial lyrics. They included the acknowledged 'big three': Calypso Rose, Singing Francine and Singing Diane.

The latter had attempted a follow-up to Francine's 1979 hit *Run Away* with her song *Ah Done Wit' Dat*, but it is not as strong either in lyrics or music as even her own sexist hit *Give It Away* in which she indicates that she is what is known internationally as an 'easy lay'. But, in *Ah Done Wit' Dat* she takes a completely different stance; she tells her violent partner she is leaving him because she can no longer tolerate the ill-treatment she has been subjected to:

> If I don't leave now
> Is licks in the morning,
> In the evening.
> I telling you flat
> I done wit' dat.

In 1979, Singing Francine attacked the subservient role which so many Caribbean women accept if they want to be regarded as 'decent' and 'respectable' in their communities. In *Run Away*, she rebukes the violent man: 'Just because you put gold teet' in she mout'/When you come home vex you licking it out' and advises the injured woman:

> Dog does run away
> Cat does run away
> Child does run away when you treating them bad
> Woman put two wheels on ya heels
> You should run away too

In earlier years, when she was the only woman calypsonian, Lady Iere had expressed similar discontent about men for whom:

> You cook dey food
> And you wash dey clothes
> When dey come home vex
> Dey does give you blows.

She warned:

> Dey got to love me or leave me
> And live wit' Miss Dorothy
> The times is too hard
> For me to keep a man that is bad.

This calypso was as popular during the early 1950s as *Run Away* was in 1979, but neither have had any impact in swaying the popular degrading and demeaning image that women have traditionally been accorded in calypso. The society as a rule has been more tolerant of the macho image of men which is projected in calypsos, such as this one by the 'Calypso Monarch' the Mighty Sparrow:

Every now and then
Knock them down
They love you long
And they love you strong
Take a piece of iron
And bruise dey knee
And then they love you
Eternally...

This was one of the most popular hits some years ago. Before that, and since then, calypsos have been sung by performers portraying women in very questionable roles. In a more recent calypso, 'human rights activist' and schoolteacher the Mighty Chalkdust informs us of his desire to see an Ayatollah take over the administration of Trinidad and Tobago. With such a leader in power, he sings, women who commit adultery would be publicly punished. No mention is made, however, of what punishment would be meted out to the men who are consenting partners in the same act.

Any woman who objects to the sexist treatment of women in calypsos encounters the argument that most other women are not bothered by it. She is told that women are the staunchest calypso fans and that the Mighty Sparrow has been most popular, during his 28 years in the field, when he produced songs relating to his sexual encounters with women.

One record shop operator even claimed that Sparrow's beautiful tribute to mothers, *A Mother Loves You Best*, has never been as popular as *The Village Ram, Everybody Go' Get, Theresa* and the most famous of his compositions, *Jean and Dinah*.

He observed,

When Sparrow sang *Education* he pointed out that education facilities were available to every little boy and girl, and he did not place a sexist image on any of these facilities. What happens? Even when people have it on an LP they don't play it. They pick out the hot, sexy numbers and this is what their children learn to sing!

He pointed out that while there were 'endless' women's organizations in Trinidad and Tobago, none of them had done what the Hindus did in 1979 and the Spiritual Baptists did in 1980—that is, complain that their image would be disrespected through public response to derogatory calypsos about them. He insisted, 'The women in Trinidad and Tobago are as a rule perfectly content with the way they are portrayed in calypso. Women have not shown overwhelming response to any calypso sung in praise of, for example; 'Netball Queen' Jean Pierre.

Traditionally, calypso has been a medium of social protest. It is time that women too use it to protest the negative image of themselves in contemporary calypsos.

Chapter 20: Sistren Women's Theatre, Organizing and Conscientization

by Honor Ford-Smith

Sistren is a theatre collective of thirteen women employed as street cleaners in the Jamaican government's Impact Programme (an employment programme). I am writing my own words here. I write 'my own words' because I want to make clear that my way of working with Sistren is conditioned by my own position on certain issues, by my own class background and by my skills in theatre. All women are oppressed, but we experience that oppression differently in both extent and form. To ignore the difference between the actresses who make up Sistren and myself is to pass over the important question of class as it affects relations between women. Second, my position on certain questions has changed in three years or so of work with the collective as outside influences on our work have altered or become stronger and as the women in Sistren have studied and taught me more about their situation. Together we evolved certain techniques which I am writing about now, here—without them—in words they would not use. These techniques are not necessarily the same that Sistren would use if they were working on their own or with another director. What I describe has grown out of the conflicts and solutions to the problems of the last years' work. They cannot be randomly applied because they are aimed at bringing about a certain process and a certain end. That end is a greater consciousness of the conditions facing women in the Caribbean. That end is the possibility of changing the structure which creates those conditions.

There would never have been a Sistren if there hadn't been an Impact Programme. I didn't consciously understand the implication of that sentence until August 1980, three years after I began working with the group. The Impact Programme had been designed to give temporary relief to the problem of unemployment. One morning in August 1980 a friend happened to mention to me that the decision to hire 10,000 women as street cleaners in the Impact Programme had been taken because of the seriousness of the unemployment situation among women. He said that it was thought that by giving the jobs to women, the wages would penetrate to the family. What I realized that morning was that in doing this, consciously or unconsciously, the PNP government had made a space within which women could begin to organize around their own concerns.

That is why Sistren spoke to me as they did when I first met them in an old, broken-down schoolhouse in Swallowfield, to talk about what we were going to do for a workers' week concert. I asked them, 'What do you want to do a play about?', and they said, 'We want to do plays about how we suffer as women. We want to do plays about how the men treat us bad'. Somehow, the Impact Programme had offered the women a chance to recognize that they shared something in common. They had a consciousness of themselves as representatives of working-class women. That first time we met, I asked them how they suffered as women and we began an exchange of experiences out of which our first piece grew. What was happening was that the group wanted to explore what they already knew, but did not know that they knew.

Downpression Get a Blow, as the first piece was called, set the tone of how the work was to proceed. One of the women in Sistren told us how she had worked in a garment factory earning a wage of twelve dollars a week. It was an American-owned factory and she and others in it were involved in trying to get better wages and better working conditions there. Women were laid off, paid off and some were fired for trying to start a union. She herself got pregnant and had to leave without maternity leave to have her baby, but she kept in touch with the other women. They managed to get outside support and just when they seemed to be getting somewhere, without a word, without a warning, the factory upped and ran away (in the middle of the night to boot). This classic example of the exploitation of women's work by runaway factories in the third world was added to, adapted and altered until it became a short play.

In those days (that was in 1977) we worked without written material until an interest in written material evolved and until we could use the scripts we had created. We selected our content from the representative experience of the women in the company. We took in material from women in the society and then later gave it back in a way which could be actively useful to others. We took old texts from life and re-entered them from a different direction— coming into the 'roles' the parts we had been asked to play, had been given to play in life—with comments.

After *Downpression*, the company asked me to go on working with them and we began a training programme at the School of Drama. At this time, we had no specific plans to continue the work in any particular direction. But during the training it became very clear that the women's lives and experiences, and the exchange of these experiences, contained a whole tradition which had not yet been openly spoken about. Further, it was also clear to me, that Sistren was able to connect to a legacy of practical art which had been so much a part of rural culture and which had afforded women an important voice in the past. In the training, at that point, it seemed important not to impose a method of work, but to create in the community of the workshop an atmosphere out of which the situation the women were discussing would emerge clearly. It was a method which would draw on a tradition which had grown out of an attempt to struggle with the powerful colonial system. It seemed that whatever was done should be done in a way that preserved and served the reality of the lives of the women in as immediate a form as possible.

123

In those first workshops I did a lot of listening to stories. I stopped trying to make things fit into improvisational methods that I had learned and started listening to stories. I recognized that the women like Sistren had delivered a cultural tradition which they now had to make use of—that in the stories they were reclaiming the institutions they had created under oppressive circumstances and which they wanted to make use of. By exploring ideas of child sharing and family support groups, the group could record a small part of the invisible historical experience of the Jamaican woman. It could also question the extent to which these traditional systems assist or impede progressive change for women. Of particular value was the establishment of a community of thought and feeling which with time and hard work would provide a context within which creative work could be structured.

It was from these considerations that *Bellywoman Bangarang* emerged. It was presented at the Barn Theatre, a commercial theatre in Kingston, because it seemed to us important that working-class women should have access to the most authoritative cultural institutions in the country, that this would make their claims visible and bring their voices to the public. There is a kind of prejudice that says that because they drudge, women from the labouring poor have no imagination. We wanted to show that this was not only a lie, but that, in fact, women from the labouring poor often have better imaginations and more poetry than bourgeois actors. *Bellywoman* exposed and confronted the society with the autobiographies of four women who were pregnant. It dealt with the way in which they had experienced motherhood and the experience of being girl children. It raised the questions of rape, domestic violence and domestic work. It showed connections between these things and unemployment and urban poverty.

After *Bellywoman* we were able to define more clearly what we were about. At that time Sistren defined itself as a collective which used (a) drama as a means to explore and analyse the events and forces that shape its members' lives and (b) theatre and workshops as a means to share this experience with other groups. It also defined itself as a group which confronted the public with issues about women which had previously been hidden or considered irrelevant. The process involved addressing the problems of the people in the collective as they defined them; it plugged these problems back into the society for discussion, for deeper analysis and for solution. This process is one of conscientization. The actresses earn a small income for their theatre and drama work and they administer the cooperative and its organization. Performances are for mixed audiences (different classes, sexes, interests), workshops for smaller, homogeneous groups.

In the workshops we find Boal's technique of 'forum theatre' to be particularly useful because it allows the group we are working with to have an immediate experience of the problem being dealt with. We present an image of the problem and then discuss it with the group. We then take apart the original image, in a step-by-step way. The audience discusses and enacts their solutions, rehearsing their new ideas. This allows the audience to take an active role in an old problem, to improvise, check the accuracy of the situation and to reimprovise. The sense of what the situation really feels like, as well as the opportunity people have to explore their capabilities, deepens the drama. At the end of a workshop like this each person has a clearer sense of what he or she can actually do to understand or change the situation.

These workshops are particularly effective with small target groups where the problem can receive more thorough treatment. Shared assumptions and experience create a sense of community and concentration and the significance of the area of experience highlighted often becomes clearer. This atmosphere can be mined very efficiently in discussion. In a workshop in the women's prison we began after a physical warm-up session to listen to a story—told to the workshop by a member of Sistren—of her experience of being forced, by a man she was afraid of, to hide stolen goods. The degree of empathy that this created among the women in prison, who had never had much opportunity to discuss their actual experiences in that way, was incredible. Each woman told her story of betrayal in a kind of spontaneous poetry born of the intensity of the situation. It was a testimony about oppression and the more women joined in, the louder was the protest. It was quite easy afterwards to discuss similarities and to search for the causes of the experiences—because gradually there was an awareness of the structural dimensions of the personal. It was possible to move from the personal to the structural analysis. This kind of experience would have been impossible in a larger audience, with a wide cross-section of people. And the understanding gained is not forgotten. The physical acting out of the communal experience, or understanding of self, seems to be very important because of the privatized nature of existence being imposed by capitalism in the third world. The empathetic response is useful only if it is based on what is true, on documentary life, on a shared class and gender consciousness. It is because Sistren draws upon the Afro-Jamaican tradition of testimony (which is an art-form but which is also real, that is, it is performed but it is not fiction) that the intellectual and the emotional impact are so strong. Workshops are never finished products. Performances to general audiences are.

Each step of the work described below attempts to broaden the basis on which the collective has contact with and expresses solidarity with the struggles of the community as a whole. What is being articulated on stage or in workshops is being struggled for, or against, in reality. The workshops with the community and the rehearsal workshops offer an opportunity for bringing together, for living study (drama), scholars, artists and poor people. What is discovered is shared through performance and then discussed with the community so that even at this stage what is learned can be reincorporated into the dramatic study (play).

Method of Work

Step 1: Physical Exercises
In the first stage the aim is to evoke themes from the group's experience.

These themes are drawn from areas in which shared experience is strongest. The early exercises aim to teach the physical skills of acting because this is the medium the group has chosen to use. The group has to become comfortable with improvisation so that it releases energy rather than restricts it. No in-depth work can go on until this happens. The work in physical skill begins with and through the body of the woman herself—it is the instrument she works with—not something introduced from outside. Initially, all work is group work, chorus work. Gradually individual work begins.

Out of these exercises certain themes will begin to emerge. The next step involves pulling out a specific theme or themes around which to continue the work. The group should pick the themes which they will use to develop their testimonies.

Step 2: Testimonies

A testimony can serve as a basis for a workshop. Or, if the team is aiming at a play-study, they can then select the testimonies which they want to explore in greater depth. The testimonies are grouped around a basic outline for a working scenario. At this stage the scenario will be very rough and incomplete. The details will become clearer, much later. In fact the final version of the scenario will probably appear to have very little relationship to the first.

In working with the testimonies it is the director's task to help the group to find connections between the testimonies they are selecting. It is also her job to help the actors to reformulate as problems the questions raised by the testimonies that will determine and deepen the course of the work. In our first year of working with testimonies, the themes which were named focused mainly on childhood and adolescence and the question of domestic work emerged very clearly as a problem. Here is an abbreviated example of an early testimony:

> I didn't get enough schooling. The reason for this: living in the country and my mother didn't have any help. She had eight of us and I was the biggest girl. She had to leave us and go out to get food. She have to work out during the day, so that she can find enough food for us. So you find that I have to stay at home most of the time and do the washing, the cooking and keep the smaller ones occupied at home. That is the reason I didn't get enough schooling. —Beverly Elliot

In reformulating this testimony as a problem, the aim is to find relationships between various areas of the problem—or between one testimony like this and another. As this happens the problem, which has now acquired a name, and the situation emerge as not just shared but as social and political. In looking at the problems in the testimony the group formulates questions about the situation and its content and these questions lead to the next stage—that of research. Some of the questions from the above testimony are, (a) why is it women's work? (b) Why did the mother have no help? In this case the answer to this question was that the father had gone to Kingston to get wage work... Which leads to another question: (c) why is wage work normally offered to men? (d) How has the movement of people from the towns to the city affected women?

Research

These questions cannot be answered from within the experience of the women only, which is where the material worked with had so far come from. The group then has to go outside to find the answers to its questions. This can be done in several ways. If we continue with the example of Bev's testimony and we try to answer the question of why wage work is normally offered to men in the form of a scene, we will very quickly see the depths of our own ignorance. At this stage we begin to read. Inevitably we will find that there is nothing to read on the question in the library—or the newspaper. So we have to call on the help of a professional researcher to work with us. The material she contributes must be in a form which the group can dramatize. The researcher is not coming in to tell the group what to do, she is coming in to offer her skills and to help answer certain questions. In another method of work the actresses from the community work with other women in their neighbourhood to collect experiences and additional material on the theme.

Having researched the problem, we can then rewrite the scenario to include discoveries from the research and to keep a sense of the questioning process which helped us to arrive at our final product. At this stage we improvise the whole scenario again.

Recording the Material

All the actresses work on recording their scenes. For Jamaican women, it is often extremely liberating to begin to write and read in the language of Creole. It is also very interesting to read one's own experiences explained and illuminated. Women, used to an oral tradition, record very accurately what they say, because the memory is often much more agile. Each person contributing to recording a scene or workshop has to delegate final responsibility to one person to put the whole thing together.

The recording and passing on of materials is an important step in the breaking down of group elitism and the sense of specialness that individual groups doing 'special' work engender. It is a way of making contact with other organizations of women among the labouring poor. The recorded material can be reused and passed on. A great deal of unrecorded improvisational work has gone on in Jamaica, and one of the sad results of this is that we have no access to material which has been done before. This obviously slows down progress. In our own experience we have also lost a great deal of our work, because of inefficiency or lack of time. In a situation where women have been 'hidden' for centuries in documents and records and planning, the recording of the play-studies and workshops becomes even more imperative.

Performance

Plays are often more vital for actors than for the audience. That is, the process of creating a play-study often is more complete for those who are doing it than for those who watch the end-product. That is why the open structure of a workshop is often more exciting and useful for both actors and participants. Nevertheless, plays receive more public attention and attract a diverse audience—which can lead to a very stimulating exchange. One of the most important things about performances is that they can be an act of solidarity with a particular issue or struggle. Sistren's *Bandoolu Version* opened in the community of central Kingston with a play performed in solidarity with the struggle of women to get maternity leave legislation passed in Jamaica.

Recently I have been experimenting with ways of making performances or play-studies into discussion-plays. That is, I have been aiming to find a structure of play which can break down into discussion and then build up into narrative or scene structure again. One of the difficulties with performances and discussion is that very often discussion appears stilted and embarrassing after the deliberate exclusion of the audience from participation in the dialogue of the play. I have been aiming for a form which melts into discussion with the audience without losing the impact that a consciously planned dialogue as well as scenario can have.

Conclusions

The process of working in drama for women involves the creating of a community in which some of the hidden or taboo subjects about women can be exposed and the audience confronted with them. As such, drama is not a reflection of life but a demystification of it, by the full exploration of these realities. After three years of work Sistren provides a dramatic forum for the problems of women from the labouring poor and in so doing helps to pressure for changes for women. By confronting what has been considered indecent, irrelevant or accepted, we have begun to make a recorded refusal of ways in which our lives have been thwarted and restricted. We have begun to refuse the forces behind those ways.

Methods and techniques are not very important. It is where they take you that matters. What becomes of the work is determined by the content and the consciousness one brings to the theme. Work of this kind can perpetuate oppressive structures as well as it can help to change them. The form is only important in so far as it structures and analyses the content and in so far as it leads to new understandings, new knowledge and new collective action.

Part 6: Women and Development

Chapter 21: New Institutions and Programmes for Caribbean Women

by Peggy Antrobus

The new awareness generated by the proclamation of a Decade for Women stimulated a number of new programmes and institutional arrangements at both regional and national levels. Women's organizations and programmes had always played an important role in Caribbean development. But before 1975, they were mainly concerned with social welfare issues. They pioneered programmes in family planning, consumer education, child care, youth work and work with the handicapped. Women had also participated actively in the movements to end slavery and colonialism and to start trade unions and political parties. The significance of 1975 was that attention was focused for the first time on the issues of equality and the contribution to development and peace. In the Caribbean, as in the other Third World countries, special attention was given to the issue of development.

The Government of Jamaica was the first, in 1974, to establish special women-oriented governmental machinery—an Adviser on Women's Affairs and a Women's Desk (later upgraded to a Women's Bureau). By 1975, Barbados, Guyana and Trinidad and Tobago had all established National Commissions on the Status of Women. Since then, similar machinery—Women's Desk, Bureaux, Commissions and Departments—has been established in all CARICOM countries.

Traditional women's organizations too responded to the Decade with a new focus on programmes intended to improve the social and economic status of women. Income-earning projects, skills-training programmes and programmes aimed at promoting a more positive self-image and wider career choices for young women were implemented alongside the more traditional programmes in day care, training in home-making skills and fund-raising for charitable causes. New leadership emerged to take up the challenge of the Decade.

Much of this energy and new initiatives at the national level were stimulated and supported by the regional programmes established within the framework of the Decade. As at national levels, those were both governmental and non-governmental. The geographic, political, social and cultural characteristics of the region provide a strong rationale for a regional approach to programmes, and the role of regional institutions, organizations and programmes are crucial for efforts at the national level.

Programmes of technical and economic cooperation between the countries of the Commonwealth Caribbean have a long history. This history finds expression in regional institutions such as the Secretariat of the Commonwealth Caribbean governments (the CARICOM Secretariat), the Caribbean Conference of Churches, University of the West Indies and countless regional associations of professionals, voluntary organizations, economic, social, sporting and cultural interests. Many international agencies have also adopted a regional approach in their assistance to the Caribbean. All of this serves to break down insularity and isolation, and to promote a movement for closer cooperation and collaboration. This characteristic is fully reflected in the field of women's programmes within the framework of the Decade.

The Caribbean Women's Association (CARIWA) started in 1970 by the wife of the Prime Minister of Guyana predated the Decade and enjoyed its highest visibility then. CARIWA is the only regional institution which provides an umbrella for all non-governmental women's groups. Most countries are represented on the Executive Committee of CARIWA by National Councils or Organizations of Women. CARIWA plays an important role in advocacy and in promoting links between women's organizations in the region. Its biennial conferences serve to highlight important regional issues as they affect women and they attempt to influence policy through their resolutions and direct lobbying of governments.

The Caribbean Conference of Churches also provides a regional focal point for church women's groups. Between 1971 (following a consultation on the Role of Women in Development) and 1982, there was a special church women's organization and programme. The women's programme of the Caribbean Conference of Churches has now been incorporated into the overall programmes of the agency, and women should benefit fully from the range of programmes including its educational and training programmes, project support, family life, youth, appropriate technology and communication programmes.

On the governmental level, three programmes can be highlighted: those of the CARICOM Secretariat, the Economic Commission for Latin America and the Caribbean (ECLAC) and the Inter-American Commission of Women (CIM) of the Organization of American States (OAS).

The CARICOM Secretariat was established by the governments of the region in 1973 to serve as a mechanism for promoting regional cooperation and collaboration. As a result of lobbying by CARIWA and supporting resolutions adopted at regional seminars and conferences, a Women's Desk was established within its programme of functional cooperation. This mechanism has led to the inauguration in 1981 of meetings of Ministers Responsible for Women's Affairs and to the convening of Inter-Agency meetings. These meetings help to promote coordination and cohesion in regional programmes. The Women's Desk of the Secretariat is mandated through the Ministerial Meetings to support and strengthen the work of national machinery.

The Economic Commission for Latin America and the Caribbean and the Inter-American Commission on the Status of Women both work to implement the Plans-of-Action adopted by government representatives at the conferences.

Both provide resources for programmes, as well as linkages with programmes of the wider systems of the UN and the OAS. Some of the established agencies have also established women's programmes within their overall scope of operations. These include the ILO, UNICEF and FAO. The special UN Voluntary Fund for the Decade has also supported a number of programmes in the region.

To complete the network of regional programmes, there is the Women and Development Unit (WAND), of the Extra-Mural Department of the University of West Indies (UWI). The establishment, objectives and programme of the WAND Unit represents the initiative and energy of women who wish to ensure that a regional institution of the importance of the University should make a contribution to the promotion of women's development programmes within the framework of the Decade.

The establishment of the WAND Unit was one of the recommendations of the regional Plan-of-Action prepared and adopted at a regional seminar on the Integration of Women in Caribbean Development held in Jamaica in 1977. The seminar was jointly sponsored by the Jamaican Women's Bureau and the Extra-Mural Department, and was attended by representatives of the governments of the English-speaking Caribbean. It was the first occasion in this region when a group of government representatives had met to give attention to the issue of women in development.

The choice of the UWI as the institutional framework for this programme was based on participants' understanding of the important role of the University in the social and economic development of the region. Its location within the Extra-Mural Department, the University's extension programme, was determined by its structure, history and philosophy of this Department. This provided the kind of autonomy and flexibility which enabled WAND to develop innovative approaches in its work and to respond to needs identified by the women of the region. At the same time, the programme was able to benefit from the resources and status of the University which is financed by the governments of the region.

Over the years of its existence the WAND Unit has worked with both government and non-government programmes and has attracted financial support from both sources at the international level. The objectives of the Unit are to build consciousness, capacity and cohesion in Women in Development programmes in this region, and its work has been crucial in the promotion and support of these important regional programmes. From its inception it recognized the importance of building awareness of the issues and this has been an important component of all its work, in training activities and project design, as well as a separate Communications Programme. The Unit's Communications Programme included the provision of communications support for field activities, as well as the use of mass media through regional channels, both print and electronic. But strategies for raising awareness go well beyond the use of the Communications Programme and included direct contact with policy-makers in key institutions and the inclusion of special sessions on the role of women in development within the training programmes of various institutions (including other Departments and Units of the UWI). At the same time, the documentation of the Unit's field experience is providing material for on-going programmes of public education, training and women's studies. Finally, the WAND Unit's use of participatory methodologies in project research, training and programme development, facilitates consciousness-raising or awareness-building as an integral part of these activities.

The more traditional academic research of other departments and units of the UWI has also made an important contribution to the growing awareness of women's issues in the region. In particular the regional research project on Women in the Caribbean (1978-81) provided important empirical data. This project was organized and directed by the Barbados branch of the University's Institute of Social and Economic Research, but included researchers from the University's campuses in Jamaica and Trinidad and Tobago, as well as from the University of Guyana. The current development of a formal programme of Women in Development Studies within the structure of teaching and research at UWI is a logical outcome of the work of the ISER and the Extra-Mural Department. The proposed programme will provide for strong linkages between teaching, research and outreach and will institutionalize the efforts of these two units since 1978.

The building of awareness is a process which needs to be continued and promoted through many channels and strategies. Awareness is a dynamic process and must accommodate inevitable changes in knowledge and perception. The process continues and will continue in the Caribbean with or without the sanctions of a special Decade for Women. One of the chief achievements of the Decade may be that it stumulated not only this new awareness of the situation of women, but helped to provide the energy, vision and resources for the establishment of the institutions and programmes which have enabled awareness to be translated into action.

Chapter 22: An Income-Generating Project for Women in Rural Jamaica

by Sonia Harris

Introduction

The close of the decade designed to effect women's greater integration into national development processes, is marked by many new questions and some significant and newly defined issues. Many of the solutions have focused over the decade on questions of equity, parity, participation and ways to generate income. We are in the unique historical position now to assess not only these quantitative gains or changes but the extent to which changes impinge on the more fundamental issue of the quality of the process of local, national or organizational management, especially when this management is exercised by women. A project in rural Jamaica has provided such an opportunity for qualitative assessment.

The project idea was born in 1980/81 out of the need repeatedly expressed to their pastor by the women in the Church, for a mechanism by which they could acquire skills and income. Many of the women already had Home Economics skills, which were informally practised as part of the Women's Federation functions. The project started in December 1981 with some 60 women from three adjoining districts (villages). Three churches provided the physical base for the women's training and production activities.

The Activities selected were:
— making straw products—for all three groups, either embroidering finished bags, hats, or making purses from straw strips.
— manufacturing garment and household articles—at the main site in Community C where goods from all three sites were also stored and sorted.
— limited beading and tie-dye work in Community A.
— baking/pastry-making—not part of the original project design but included later to supplement income in Community B.

The Structure was hierarchical in design and the minister at the head of the pinnacle was the sole male to whom most project members looked for direction and final decisions. He was ably assisted by a management team of women, including a financial secretary and production manager who were coordinated

135

by his wife. These were women of long-standing prestige and status within the community.

The next level—that of instructors and those understudying instructors and managers—was the most dynamic element, where mobility could take place within an otherwise rigid structure. The workers, or producer-trainees, made up the bulk of the project participants—approximately 80% at project inception, or 50 of the original 60 women; and 66% by year 2, by which time some 30 participants had dropped out. New members, many young, were recruited in year 2, especially at the main site, but it is a core of older women who have survived the project experience with patience and dignity.

Contemporary Socio-Cultural & Economic Context of the Women's Lives

The women, particularly the older ones, were born in a rural environment, at the centre of which was a sugar estate, still in private hands after some four hundred years. This estate was the single largest employer of labour from six surrounding districts (including project districts) from the early 1500s until the 1950s, when the Tourist Industry began to rival it. These two industries provide a historical backdrop to the women's lives, especially indicating the transition which has occurred in the world-view of the older generation *vs* that of the younger.

In neither case were blacks (peasants, folk) in control of these industries. Similarly, women-owned businesses were unheard of during this period. Rather, males—mulattos, local whites and expatriate whites—dominated the economy, even as it went through the transition from a rural agricultural to an urban tourist-centred one. This situation still obtains.

The peasantry improved their status over the past hundred years independently of these two industries, by means of

land purchase and ownership (including cattle rearing, rather than mere subsistence agriculture, and medium-sized (average ten acres) coconut, cane or banana farms;
and educating its sons and daughters to the professional positions formerly denied them.

It was not unusual during the turn of the century period for women to own or inherit land and to pass it on to female offspring.

The church and its related functions and responsibilities created its own system of professionalism and leadership. An ambitious young rural male, with many avenues to professional life closed, could look to the ministry as a source of employment and status. The proliferation of churches in rural Jamaica attests to this. Teachers, shopkeepers, nurses and doctors and dressmakers formed a core of other professionals, to which many women could aspire.

Of the three groups in the project, participants' families in Community A, the more remote hill-side one, relied more on independent trades and agriculture, creating an internal self-sufficiency in quiet resistance to the extended slavery status of many workers on the sugar estate. Six of seven participants there were part of farm families or earned from practising an independent trade. Only one worked for the sugar estate.

Families in Community B and C have become more professional than A and the area boasted a few women doctors and a middle-income group, which complemented its fundamental agricultural structure. At the same time, more sugar-estate workers came from Communities B and C than A, indicating for those two areas a mixed independent semi-professionalism with dependency links to the estate and hotels. Many families of the participants in this combined area were part of the informal agricultural sector (13 of 21 or 63%); the managers were part of the middle-income group; and some (28%) especially spouses, worked either on the sugar estate or in the tourist industry. Another few, unlike Community A, work as domestics.

There were, however, erosions since the 1950s into the self-sufficiency described, particularly by non-project members of Community A. This was due to the permanent migration to the main town—some fifteen miles away—in search of more glamorous work than agriculture, especially by youth, whose aspirations have continued to rise since the post World War II period; out-migration to the UK (and to a lesser extent to the US) which removed some of the more enterprising and skilled people from their communities, and reduced the number of models of assertiveness, male and female on which community stability was based. These factors have greatly influenced the project participants' view of themselves and of the most expedient route to upward mobility, especially for their children.

It is evident, if we study recent Caribbean history, that significant *external* factors have destroyed the fabric of community life and community economies after World War II. These include:

(a) *Tourism*, which was imposed on the people and unevenly accelerated the pace of the people's development. People responded by reducing the time and effort spent working for themselves and increased the time spent working for others. The hotel industry was not planned around the needs of the local people by stimulating or organizing of local food production, but depended on imports for the bulk of food, to maintain the tastes of the international visitors. This was another blow to the budding entrepreneurship within these three rural communities.

(b) *Migration* possibilities to the UK were opened up by virtue of more liberal immigration laws which, after the war, gave all Commonwealth citizens full rights of entry and residence in the UK. Hundreds of thousands of Jamaicans abandoned their farms and shops, to barter their skills on what they saw as the higher priced European market. The pull factor in this case exerted as much pressure on the people as did the factors pushing them out.

(c) A third factor, *political centralization*, led to excesses on the part of the politicians during this same period; after self-government in 1944, they began to make increasingly inappropriate promises, about areas of responsibility formerly assumed by communities. Thus, institutionalized party-aligned competitiveness over artificial resources was induced, and the self-help quality of rural life gradually destroyed.

The pattern of ownership, control and influence in these communities has remained outside of the hands of small folk, as far as large properties are concerned. The Department of Statistics in Jamaica indicates in its Land Distribution Tables that, although small farmers (owning ten acres or less) in the parish where the project is located own approximately 25% of the total number of farms, these farms represent less than 5% of the total acreage in the parish. So that the exercise of power and decision-making that would affect an entire parish did not rest in the hands of the majority of small farmers. Although skills in management and farm- and market-related decisions did exist among them, these were ignored when the development process made a leap towards pseudo-industrialization. Women were left even further behind in this process and sought work in hotels at menial wages to supplement farm income.

The women, though always affected by socio-economic forces, are now better able than two years ago, because of the project experience, to analyse these factors. Entering into the market economy and learning how forces operate there has enabled them to analyse even the impact of the IMF (International Monetary Fund) loan to Jamaica, on the pricing structure here and on their lives. This growing sophistication in analysis and the expanding consciousness of these rural women may be the single most significant impact of the project on the women's lives.

Analysis of Project Related Issues

Politics of Development
There is obvious merit in building a project on the strengths that exist in a community. In this case, reinforcing a women's group, the Women's Federation from the church, by forming a project around them, points to not so much the inherent success built-in to women-only projects, but the capacity of women to organize, centralize and produce if they have a sense of direction. Seventy percent of the women in the first quarter and 50% at the last quarter had been members of the Women's Federation or Youth arm, some for as long as eighteen years. The fact that the group size later fell from 60 to 30, actually reduced the tensions and conflicts within the group and helped the core of women remaining, to identify more closely with the management process.

The group in Community B, which also did baking, has demonstrated among the six regular women there, all older, that a small-sized cohesive group, which employs a democratic form of management, can work in a non-competitive productive manner. Aside from size and composition of group, the project also applied an incentive strategy at the end of year 2 to reward and encourage the women as they went into the new phase of self-management. This approach was timed for Christmas, came at a critical transition juncture and could if used more consciously as a built-in reinforcement, lead to permanent development gains.

The use of information to educate rather than to manipulate was not sufficiently explored, nor were training seminars offered often enough to broaden the range of skills, ideas and new thoughts which could be filtered into a partially closed church community.

Institutional Framework

The church, which formed the institutional framework within which the project took place, played different roles in the project members' lives, including the following:

(1) *A spiritual role*, guiding both the personal belief system (and world-view) of the women, as well as determining the form of their organized religion.
(2) *A social role*, through the Women's Federation and Christmas parties, which provide the women an opportunity to socialize, to please their minister with their cooking and to organize some of their talents and skills.
(3) *an economic and productive role* meeting the income and training needs of the women through the project.

In these ways, the church has not limited its role, or the use of its facilities, to the spiritual but has tried to meet the more practical needs of its members and of the community as a whole. The planning of these activities, though initiated and carried out by their minister, are organized and managed largely by the women themselves.

A further observation is that the participants sense of church affiliation had more meaning to them than their community affiliation.

Empowerment of Women

This delicate process can be measured in the following broad areas:

- self-image of members
- productive roles of the women
- reproductive role and attitudes of women
- changes in family/community
- self/group management potential within the group
- emerging leadership within the group

The acquisition of a new skill has done much to enhance the self-image of many of the women. Only among a few, who were slow or were not encouraged to sew on the machine, was there any evidence in year 2 of the inferiority quality common to some unskilled rural women. The sophistication of many of the women in analysing socio-political issues is indicative of the self-assurance that I have seen grow within group members over the two-year period.

Coupled with the new skills is the organization of new productive roles for the women. Only 4 of 28 (14%) interviewed in year 2 reported earning steady income from formal work before joining the project. However, their new productive roles have not guaranteed the empowerment of the entire group but only of individuals within it.

As a group, the members of Community B display a quiet sense of power management in that they have an independent area of activity—the baking of pastry, of which they control the purchasing, marketing and budgeting of the product and profits. Decisions made about the sharing of profits among themselves at the end of year 2 may not have been in their long-term interest and were not pleasing to the Project Managers—but they were *their* decisions.

In Community A, much of the power management potential which was evident in year 1 has been stifled or not cultivated. They have the least control of the three groups over the productive process. All references to this group, including the minister's, indicate that Group A has only been prepared to supply the central collecting house at Community C with goods when required. The initiative which a few members from Community A showed early in the marketing area went unrecognized and members have retreated, especially in light of the irregularity of their work, to a more complacent role within the project.

Project members in Community C, though equipped with the most valuable market skill of garment manufacturing, have not, as a group, been encouraged to make decisions. While they can decide individually on designs that go on some items, it is their manager who demonstrates, as a case example, the process of self-empowerment, which is a much less complex, though admirable, process than that of empowerment of the group.

Whereas most of the project members report that their mothers had nine, eleven or sixteen children, the older members interviewed in year 1 had an average of 4.7 children and the younger ones had none. In year 2, only one of the seven mostly new young members had two children, ages six and four years. That mother at 23 years typifies the view of all young people interviewed, who do not want more than two children. She says that if she gets married she would have one more, but otherwise wants none.

Although 2 of the 28 women interviewed in year 2 had eight and ten children respectively, all the others had small or medium-sized families. They felt strongly that the country was over-populated and they would not encourage their children to have more than two. The distribution of children by group is as follows:

— 6 persons interviewed in Community A have 24 children or a mean of 4 children per person
— 6 persons interviewed in Community B have 22 children or a mean of 3.7 children
— 10 persons interviewed in Community C have 22 children or a mean of 2.2 children
— 6 young persons had no children

In total 22 respondents had 68 children or 3 children per respondent. The majority of respondents, however, had at least two extra children—nieces, nephews, step-children or grand-children—living with them.

Aspirations for themselves and especially for their children show a movement away from child-bearing and labouring in the fields to wanting their offspring to have fewer children and 'come out good' in terms of their productive role. Migration out of the area is seen as a good thing if opportunities seem to exist elsewhere.

Family members have been supportive of the women's participation in the project, though if the women began to command a high income or seriously manage the project as a cooperative business, the response, of spouses especially, might not be so positive.

A core of women have stuck with the project in spite of negative comments from a few family and community members that the project is 'a waste of time'. These are the women who measure their personal development not just in monetary terms but in the acquisition of new skills which they feel could be a buffer for them if times got harder and they had to work for themselves.

The channel for expression of the self-management potential within the group is complicated by the project's built-in hierarchical structure which participants seem to accept. Whereas this channel is open in their own home production and trading activities outside the project [approximately 20% of the present group still sell their agricultural produce in the market], within the project they accede to the authority of instructors and managers. Only 4 of 28 or 14% of participants are involved in purchasing or marketing even at the level of making suggestions. This varies, however, between groups. Community C has the least freedom to sell products, and is the most dependent on the overall initiatives in the management area controlled mostly by two women. As individuals, the members of each group are free to choose, within prescribed limits, the designs that go on a product. Production lines are, however, determined primarily by the manager in response to orders or market trends that she receives or observes. Group decisions around new ideas are not evident, though the manager and marketing officer (commission arrangement) confer regularly.

The instructor in Community A will show some assertiveness in selling goods to passers-by from the project site. The response from community members is often positive—this is the same community that had a history of self-sufficiency. The members of Community B, because of their baking, have total control over this one aspect of their production.

The management potential is there within each of the older women, who describe a situation of sole control or mostly joint control with spouse around domestic matters, as well as around home enterprises such as chicken-and egg-rearing, agricultural production, or sewing.

It is the younger women who show limited self-management skills. The potential in them for independent and creative thought has never been cultivated within the authoritarian education system to which they were exposed. Within the project, therefore, they do not question, challenge or suggest.

In summary, the self/group management potential within the groups is hampered by:

— the unfulfilled aspirations of the women to be nurses, policewomen or teachers, and the lack of preparation for the productive roles they now play within the project.

— structural boundaries or role specifications built into the project design which do not allow for free flow of ideas throughout the groups.

— the absence of a deliberate incentive strategy directed at encouraging young people to participate, first at the level of ideas, in the running of the project, as part of their training for leadership and future management.

Leadership roles had been formerly defined within the Women's Federation groups and have largely been transferred to the project through a selection process determined by the minister and his wife. Some mobility has occurred for a few women. For example, because the instructors for the straw group at Community A and C dropped out (or were phased out) two women who may not have otherwise had the opportunity became instructors. One is virtually self-taught, as the former instructor showed her very little, and the other who could sew a little before, has learned quickly from other instructors about straw and beading work.

However, the leadership structure is more closed than open and informal leadership training of understudies provides the only avenue for practising the skills of management.

Within the closed structure, there are however some dynamic features. For example, the creativity and accomplishment of the production manager and marketing person are a model for the other women, whether the leadership system within the project becomes open to them or not.

The process of gaining control of the project is a complex one. Based on the project design and the traditional roles played by people in authority in Jamaica, it was difficult for those 'in charge' to identify the strategies needed to break into the culture of poverty which has denied ownership and control to the majority of people.

Many suggestions were made to me from early in the first year by participants, some of whom have dropped out, as to ways to enhance the marketing of their goods. Suggestions such as 'sending more people out to sell more things', 'advertising more', 'putting up posters', 'putting a sign at the gate', 'having a bazaar', were never fed back into the management system. Thus a moment was lost to incorporate even one of those ideas into the marketing system and show participants that their involvement was valued and compensate them for the low income received.

In one large meeting held during the first year participants were asked to write down how they felt about the project. The majority said glowing things about the project; interestingly this came at the height of brewing discontent in the project. At no point were the participants asked to make suggestions as to how the project could be improved. So the participants' needs for more involvement in planning and decision-making, though stated, were largely ignored.

The educational level of managers and workers contributed to the different sense of ownership that both groups felt towards the project. The fact that management controlled the finances in the project and information vital to the women's sense of involvement caused the dependency relationship and power imbalance to be extended. There is little evidence that the majority of participants felt that the project was theirs. Even the instructor in charge of the group at Community B waited weeks to get permission from the minister to fix a sewing machine, used for making straw goods, rather than going ahead and getting her group's approval. On the other hand, this same group was able to gain control over some productive resources and manage a significant part of project activities themselves through their baking—though this was not intended as part of the project design. Through this, we can measure the factors leading to control of the productive process. It is a vital lesson for project managers who find it difficult to share ownership meaningfully with participants. For the baking activities, the group buys its own flour and sugar in bulk, transports it on the bus, bakes and markets it themselves, keeps its own records and bank account, and shares profits when and how they see fit.

Many members, especially in Community A and C, see themselves as workers and compare benefits gained in previous or alternate employment, in for example, the hotel industry. The project was seen as belonging to the managers, who set direction and made decisions. The workers worked for them. The members were told, however, by the last quarter that the project was theirs, though financial control remained with the director, coordinator and financial secretary. It is as this situation changes that a new sense of ownership could be instituted.

Overall Impact of Project on Women's Lives
The project had a positive impact on the women's lives in the following areas:
(1) Skill transfer and an increasing sense of confidence because of the new skill.
(2) Exposure to outside development agents—national and extra-national.
(3) Independence born of income earnings, albeit small, which allowed the women, especially those who had not had steady income before, to make more of their own decisions on expenditure. Almost 80% made their own decisions around spending the money they earned. Money is usually used, however, in the home or on children especially for school expenses.
(4) New status within the family, as they now had the regular responsibility of going to work. The spouses, particularly of the more active women, seemed outwardly proud and supportive of their wives' accomplishments, though three of them were laid off their jobs sometime before the project started. Only 5 of 28 participants (18%) depended on their husbands' income alone. For another 33%, project earnings were the families' main source of income.
(5) A growing sense of solidarity within the groups which transcended the class and age barriers separating workers from management. This sense of unity, seen in the orderly way that work was carried out, became a stable feature of the group, particularly after the ones who had conflicts within the group dropped out. Competitive feelings, though occasionally expressed, were

kept to a minimum.

(6) A growing concern for their daughters' educational prospects, even more than their sons (44% wanted 'a good education' for their daughters and 33% for their sons), in recognition of the role that education plays in a woman's life.

(7) As mentioned earlier, a consciousness-raising process has been quietly at work in this project, to the point where even the fluctuations of international market forces began to take on more and more meaning in the women's lives. They have said that 'people with money do not want the things that they make'.

The project had a mixed or negative impact on their lives for the following reasons:

(1) The devaluing worth of the Jamaican dollar created tensions and anxieties about money, even though nearly 50% of those interviewed said they joined the project to learn a skill, compared to 25% who were interested in earning money from the project. (The other 25% were doing nothing before they joined.) Participants spoke freely of the hardships they had in gaining access to needed goods and services. One woman told of taking $20 earned from the project to the grocery shop and found that it bought only four small items, which frightened her. The project at no time addressed the question of increasing the piecework rate (approx. $1-1.50 per straw item) though the dollar was worth, at the end of the project, half of what it was worth at project inception.

(2) The project may be reinforcing some inferiority feelings, especially around class, education and age factors, rather than helping everyone to grow at an equal pace.

(3) The feeling that Community A was 'the shakiest group' did not change over the two-year period, and references like 'jealous child' or 'step-child' were humorously made to them. Assertiveness expressed in this group in year 1 met with no encouragement and year 2 found even the assertive ones saying they liked the structure with the present managers in charge and did not want that to change.

Project Groups Compared to Community

The project group can be compared to other groups in the wider community in the following ways:

(1) It is unusual for a church to extend its activities to include economic activity and to extend use of its facilities, usually unavailable to community programming for six days per week, in new, practical and productive ways. Participants are thus being exposed to an expanded role of the church, from which they draw benefits.

(2) The project provides participants with a unique opportunity for the young and elderly to work together, thus addressing a growing gap between the generations. This approach has only been used in one other national programme.

(3) The project enables participants to expand their world view, to secure opportunities in education for themselves and offspring and to meet and share ideas with people, local and foreign, who are concerned with the

development of women.

(4) The project may, however, over-structure the experience of maturation for the young members, offer them a false or unrealistic level of aspirations and prevent the normal individual or group exploration of options (though limited) available outside of the project. The dropping out of young people in each of the three groups without giving a reason may indicate their readiness to explore life for themselves outside the confines of the adult or church world.

General Characteristics of the Project

The project has been characterized over the two year period by the following significant factors:

Negative:

(1) Ambiguity within the structure and therefore in the outcome. For example, initiative among members broadly was not encouraged, as that could have threatened the established order, yet at the beginning of year 3, one manager complained about the women's 'not wanting to go out and explore markets, but expecting someone to do it for them'.

(2) Entrenched attitudes of members around patriarchy, educational standing and authority. Whereas the Baptist church has a history of revolutionary fight against colonialism and oppression (Sam Sharpe Baptist Deacon—National Hero, 1860), once the local order was established, female members especially succumbed to a new form of benevolent male domination.

(3) The focus in the project on a women's centred approach was insufficient, as a change strategy in an authoritarian structure. Addressing issues of equality, parity and income distribution through such a project design does not automatically lead to development. Rather, within the process and within the quality of interaction could be seen attitudes and behaviours which perpetuated inequality and disparity especially around the exercise of authority and rewards.

Although deliberate strategies, such as the understudy arrangement, were used to ensure some mobility for the women, the project's overall weakness was that it lacked a focus on development and a philosophy which could guide a system of democratic management and self-evaluation.

(4) The consumption habits of the past thirty years have meant that young people have not been taught to support local industry. They see local, rural goods as inferior to those made abroad or in the cities. Products made in the project are not sufficiently used by the participants themselves as an example to others, yet tourists and members of the community are expected to buy them. New and creative ways of designing, adapting or promoting products were not considered.

Positive:

(1) The project design's most positive aspect is its use of human resources

145

from within its own communities. The project director, coordinator, financial secretary, production managers and instructors are *all* from within their own boundaries.

This factor alone qualifies this project as a model of rural enterprise, which could be duplicated in many communities island-wide, with the necessary adaptations in the process of management.

(2) The quiet forward growth of Group B and the movement of select members of Group C, including the acquisition of negotiation skills in the marketing area, represent just some in a range of accomplishments for the project women. These individuals and group B, are personal models of entrepreneurship for the larger community.

Implications for Policy

Policy-makers could draw the following lessons from this project:

(a) Pre-planning with project participants has a direct and positive bearing on outcome.

(b) Training inputs that go beyond the technical area, and include relationships, process monitoring and power sharing management-training can lead to qualitatively richer results.

(c) The creativity of producers can be best released when questions dealing with self-acceptance and powerlessness are resolved.

(d) An educational and promotional strategy was needed to market products, matched with an analysis of what people can be encouraged to buy and why.

(e) A community building focus and goal can lead to more permanent change, even for those not directly involved in the project, than obtains with a narrow project focus, which can further complicate community tensions and jealousies.

Through this project, however, the emphasis on promoting and improving the organizational and management capabilities of women, has resulted in a greater use of human resources and has led to the beginning of building up community economies.

Chapter 23: From Silent Beneficiaries to Active Participants

by Pat Ellis

Introduction

The voices of women at the community level are seldom heard at the national level, and their specific needs and problems are not usually incorporated into national development plans. One strategy for influencing policy is through the implementation, documentation and evaluation of pilot projects. The underlying assumption is that pilot projects implemented at the community level can test the use of certain approaches and will promote the full participation of rural women in every phase of the development process. Within such micro-projects, factors which prohibit rural women's full participation in the development process can be identified. These factors include: women's low self-esteem and lack of confidence; lack of recognition of women's contribution to the social and economic development of their communities and societies; lack of an understanding of the changing roles and relationships between women and men; and, women's low level of participation in the decision-making process.

A pilot project which uses a participatory methodology and focuses on the concerns of rural women can demonstrate how the 'bottom-up approach' to development can facilitate a greater degree of participation by these women in the process of rural development. The Pilot Project for the Integration of Women in Rural Development which was implemented in Rose Hall, St Vincent, in 1980, has clearly demonstrated this. Rose Hall is a small rural community on the northern, leeward side of the island of St Vincent. It nestles among the mountains 1,232 ft above sea-level. The majority of its fifteen hundred people are engaged in some aspect of agricultural production.

The women of Rose Hall are faced with the same problems as many poor rural women in other parts of the Caribbean: hard, long hours of work, low income, insufficient to meet the needs of their family, lack of adequate child-care and other facilities and lack of access to a variety of resources. The women of Rose Hall, however, have a strong potential for leadership, a sense of purpose, an enthusiasm and a willingness to work to improve their situation and that of their families—and the Pilot Project has provided them with the opportunity to achieve their goals.

Within this Pilot Project many of the issues which affect women's participation in the development process have been highlighted. The people of Rose Hall have examined these issues and have gained a better understanding of how and why women, as well as the entire community, are affected when such issues are not addressed. As a result they have planned and implemented a number of action projects and programmes in order to change this situation, to remove some of the constraints, and to facilitate greater participation of the women in the development of the community.

How have they been able to do this, and what are some of the factors which have led to the many positive outcomes of their efforts?

Readiness for Change

Perhaps the most important factor is that the people of Rose Hall were 'ready for change'. Moreover, they not only felt the need for change, but they understood that the power to change was in their own hands; what is more important, they were willing to take any action which they felt was necessary to achieve this change.

Secondly, the people in Rose Hall realized from the beginning that change/development is a long and slow process, that it does not happen overnight, and that it must be planned. In the words of one woman during a meeting in the early stages of the project, 'Yes, we need a lot of things right now, but we have to wait until everything is planned out.' The people of Rose Hall have been consistent in their planning and organizing of community projects and programmes. They have developed, and continue to go through, a process of participatory planning which allows a large number of community members to be involved in deciding which programmes and projects should be implemented and how.

Over the life of the project certain characteristics have emerged which seem to be of critical importance in projects which seek to facilitate greater participation of women (and indeed of all members of rural communities) in the process of rural development. These are:

1. Involvement in research activities.
2. Provision of broad based non-formal education and training programmes.
3. Development of action programmes and projects to meet specific needs.
4. The involvement and support of men (and children).
5. Community mobilization and collective action.

As the project has progressed, the women in Rose Hall have been fully involved in all of these areas of activity. They have benefited not only on an individual level, but have been responsible for many of the positive outcomes, both tangible and intangible which have benefited the entire community.

A brief look at these five areas of activity in Rose Hall will give an idea of how both the level and nature of women's participation has improved over a period of two-and-a-half years.

Research Activities

Before the Pilot Project, like many other women in rural communities in the Caribbean, the only knowledge that the women of Rose Hall had of research was in their role as the 'objects of research'. They had provided answers to dozens of questions on questionnaires developed by 'researchers' who were collecting information on practically every aspect of their lives and families but, as is usually the case in this traditional approach to research, these women had no idea what happened to the information after they had given it. They had not heard of it since, neither had they had access to it.

When they became involved in the Pilot Project they began to understand their situation, and identify their needs and problems. As they explored possible solutions to some of these problems, they began to realize that they needed a great deal of information before they could plan specific programmes and projects. On their own initiative they have set about getting the information that they needed. In essence, they have applied the principles of participatory research.

They usually collect 'general' information from the community at large by conducting community surveys and organizing community meetings. They then collect specific, more detailed information from particular interest groups (such as mothers of pre-school children) and individuals by means of group discussion and individual indepth interviews, some of which they have taped. The information which they collect is then analysed and 'fed back' to the community via role play, skits, drawing and other creative media, in a large community meeting. Both the information which is collected and the views expressed in the community meetings are then used as the basis to develop programmes or projects. An adult education programme and a pre-school project are two projects which have been developed as a direct result of this type of research.

Throughout, the women are in control of the research process. They decide what is to be researched, what kind of and how much data they need, what methods they will use to collect it, and how and for what they will use the data which they have collected. In this way research, rather than being an end in itself, has become a tool which the people of Rose Hall use to facilitate their own development and that of their community.

Community Based Non-Formal Education and Training

Over the last two years the women in Rose Hall have been involved in a process of education and training. Early in the project a number of women, members of the project working group, participated in a three-week training workshop in Participatory Approaches to Community Needs Assessment, Programme Planning and Evaluation. By participating in a series of structured activities, they learnt how to use techniques like role play, drawing, photographs, poetry, charts and group discussion to identify and analyse situations and problems, and to explore how skills and resources within the community could be harnessed to deal with these. They realized—some of them for the first time— that *they* had skills and capabilities which they could use to change and improve their situation if they so wished. However, as they began to plan and develop programmes and projects they also realized that they needed additional skills and knowledge for them to assume leadership roles and for their efforts to succeed.

They have initiated a series of training workshops and seminars in personal development, interpersonal relationships, problem-solving techniques, programme planning, project development, proposal writing, evaluation and small business management. In addition, some women have received training in such practical skills as sewing, food preparation and preservation, record-keeping and improved agricultural practices. The adult education programme which they developed and implemented in late 1981 is still in progress with classes being held twice a week.

The women themselves decided on the content and form, as well as on the timing and duration of the workshops and classes, and although they have used outside resource persons occasionally the majority of resource persons for these education programmes have been people in the community—mainly female teachers. These have received additional in-depth training in the art and methods of teaching adults, of teaching literacy to adults and of preparing materials for this purpose. They have used non-formal education methods to draw on the experience of learners and to involve the women in a teaching learning process in which each learner sees herself also as a teacher sharing her knowledge and skills.

As a result of this broad-based community education programme the women have experienced feelings of greater self-worth and self-esteem. They have gained in self-confidence and are displaying a greater desire and willingness to accept leadership positions and to actively participate in decision-making both in their families and in their wider community. Moreover, many are using the practical skills and knowledge which they have acquired to manage their household tasks and time more efficiently and to increase or supplement their family income.

Development of Action Programmes and Community Projects

The Rose Hall Community Working Group is made up of approximately thirty members, three-quarters of whom are women. This group has been responsible for planning, developing and implementing a number of community projects within the last two years, which have been of benefit to many women. In October 1981 they began an adult education programme to increase knowledge and skills in agricultural information and home improvement, and to upgrade the literacy level of community members. Those women who have been attending adult classes are now making better use of local foods because of the new and interesting food preparation and presentation techniques which they have learned. The nutritional status of some families has improved considerably since the women have become aware of the importance of balanced meals and of the need to include more protein in their diet. Some women are now raising chickens so as to increase the protein intake of family members, while others are selling chickens and eggs to supplement and increase the family income.

The Working Group organized a sewing project in July 1982 to provide uniforms for school children in the village. This has saved many mothers from travelling to the capital, Kingstown, 23 miles away, to purchase material and then to pay to have uniforms made. Because the group was able to get a loan to buy material in bulk, it was in a position to offer the completed uniforms to parents at a reasonable price. This resulted in considerable savings to many mothers—especially those with more than one child—and in a sense of pride among people in the village when the children turned out to school in the new uniforms. One parent expressed his sentiments this way, 'I feel good when I see Rose Hall's children in their uniforms—they look so smart!'

Concerned about the proper care and education of young children in the community, the group has planned a pre school project. The pre school was started in February 1983 and caters for 30 of the 72 children between two-and-a-half to five years. The parents of these children meet regularly with the two teachers and members of a pre-school committee to discuss topics relating to the development and care of young children.

The Working Group was also instrumental in organizing a farmers' group whose total membership is now between 65-70 persons, one-third of whom are women. Through the farmers' group women have gained more direct access to farm supplies—seeds and equipment—and to extension personnel and senior officials in the Ministry of Agriculture. They are benefiting from a fertilizer scheme which the farmers' group is operating and, by means of visits to other farmers and agricultural stations in other parts of the island, their knowledge about agricultural practices has increased. In all of these projects women have been at the forefront and they have been involved at every stage in the decision-making process. They are both active contributors as well as beneficiaries of the development which is taking place in their village.

The Involvement of Men

If women are to realize their full potential and be free to develop as human beings, then it is important for their men to understand this and to accept that women should not be denied this right. Instead of passively accepting the idea of male dominance and female subordination, women and men need to understand and accept the concepts of interdependence and mutual respect.

In spite of the fact that emphasis within the Pilot Project was on women and their role in rural development, the men of Rose Hall have been involved from the beginning. A few men are members of the Working Group, and there is at least one man on every project committee. Men have also participated in various training workshops and seminars. Women and men meet regularly to share ideas, discuss community problems and explore solutions together. Men are listening to the women and are gaining new insights into how their women think and feel.

The women of Rose Hall realize that they need the support of the men and that more should be involved in the various community activities, which they are implementing. In July 1982 they invited the men to a special workshop to discuss the role of men in the development of Rose Hall. In this workshop couples talked with each other, identified problems which they were facing and analysed some of the causes for problems between the sexes. They also assessed the effect that the Pilot Project was having on them as individuals, on their family and on their community as a whole. Some of the men present gave concrete examples of how their spouses' involvement in the project was benefiting them and their families. One man remarked that he was 'seeing signs of improvement in my home'; another agreed that the project was providing opportunities for the women to use their talents; and yet another pledged to support and encourage his wife's development—'I will stay at home and make supper on some evenings so that Joan can go to classes!'—this he does, as do many others.

As the dialogue between the sexes continues, communication barriers are being broken down and the quality of interpersonal relationships and of family life is steadily improving. 'I am overcoming many situations now when I take time to reason with my wife', said one husband. There is a spirit of cooperation and camaraderie in the village as women and men work alongside each other to achieve common goals of personal and community development.

Community Mobilization

From the early stages of the Pilot Project the community accepted and took responsibility for its implementation. A Community Committee for Women and Development was formed and its members, representatives of existing organized community groups, were responsible for coordinating and implementing project activities. This Committee later became the Community Working Group and its members have increased from the original 16 to approximately 35.

In order to ensure that its ideas, suggestions and plans for projects and programmes are meeting community needs, and that a large cross-section of community members are actively involved, the Working Group has developed informal and formal mechanisms which ensure continuous dialogue. They have informal discussions with individuals and groups on a continuous basis and they organize community meetings on a regular basis. Mass community meetings are now a common feature and form an integral part of a process of community participatory decision-making. These meetings are usually attended by about seventy persons, all of whom participate actively in discussions.

Community meetings may be organized by the Working Groups to exchange information, to get opinions on and to discuss new project ideas, to discuss critical issues or problems which community members are facing, to plan strategies for tapping resources from government and non-governmental agencies, and generally to decide on what action the community will take in order to achieve common goals. The consensus arrived at during these community meetings becomes the basis for action, so that whenever the Working Group speaks or acts it is sure of the support of community members, because it speaks with the voice of the community.

This process of community dialogue, participatory decision-making and collective action has empowered the people of Rose Hall and has enabled them to 'speak in a strong voice' to policy makers and planners at the national level in St Vincent. They have written letters and sent delegations to various government ministries, they have had visits from 'high officials', to see for themselves and to discuss with the villagers; they have received assistance, advice, materials and human resources for their many community programmes and projects. On one occasion, when the group requested the use of a vacant room in the primary school to start a nursery school until they could acquire a separate building, the headteacher and some members of staff refused to give permission. When a series of meetings with the staff members proved fruitless, a community meeting was called to discuss the matter. About seventy-eight people attended the meeting and after discussing the issues at great length their consensus was: 'We need a pre-school for our children, the primary school is in our village to serve our children, there is space available in the school, we need the space, the space is there, we must get the space!' They all agreed that a petition should be drawn up and that they would all sign it and send it to the Ministry of Education. However, this was not necessary, for shortly afterwards, faced with this kind of community pressure, the headteacher agreed to let the vacant room be used for the nursery classes.

Conclusion

Because the pilot project included components of research, education and training, action programmes and projects it has been able to systematically confront the particular needs of women and the issues which affect their participation in the development process. Furthermore, because it involved not only women but other community members—men—it facilitated a process of dialogue and participatory decision-making which has resulted in the mobilization of the community for collective action to achieve common goals.

Consequently, the women of Rose Hall now have a voice—a strong voice which is being heard and being listened to—not only in their own community, but beyond.

Appendix 1: Resources Available to Caribbean Women

Regional Institutions and Organizations

Caribbean Community (CARICOM)
CARICOM is an inter-governmental association of governments in the Caribbean region. It provides a mechanism through which heads of governments and government ministries meet to discuss, decide and cooperate on matters of mutual concern in various fields such as education, health, trade and women's affairs. The Secretariat headquarters is in Georgetown. The Caribbean Women's Desk for the Integration of Women in Development established in 1981 is headed by Ms Magda Pollard, Women's Affairs Officer.

Contact Address: CARICOM Secretariat
                     PO Box 10827
                     Georgetown, Guyana.

Caribbean Women's Association (CARIWA)
CARIWA is a regional umbrella organization for non-governmental women's groups in the Caribbean. It has a membership of over 500 women's groups from 12 countries. It meets biannually and initiates and promotes and facilitates a wide variety of programmes and projects that aim at improving the economic and social well being of women.

Contact Address: Ms Neva Edwards
                    Secretary CARIWA
                    c/o The Social Centre
                    PO Box 16
                    13 Turkey Lane
                    Ros'eau, Commonwealth of Dominica.

Women and Development Unit (WAND)
Established in 1978, WAND is part of the Extra-Mural Department, University of the West Indies. The Unit's programme includes the provision of technical assistance and training to women's groups in the region, the production and dissemination of a wide range of materials on and for women in the region, and the development and implementation of indepth projects that focus on the full integration of women in the development process. In all of its work,

WAND uses a participatory method.

Contact Address: Peggy Antrobus
Tutor Coordinator
WAND
Extra-Mural Department, UWI
The Pine
St Michael, Barbados.

Women's Studies Groups, UWI
On each of the main campuses of the University of the West Indies, there is a women's studies group. The aim of these groups is to stimulate debate and to work towards the introduction of women's studies courses within the various faculties. Each group, headed by a campus coordinator, organizes seminars, workshops, and symposia, promotes and encourages research on and by women and collects documents, develops and disseminates relevant material.

Contact Address: 1) Kathleen Drayton
School of Education
University of the West Indies
Cave Hill
St Michael, Barbados.

2) Hermoine McKenzie
Department of Sociology
University of The West Indies
Mona
Kingston 7, Jamaica.

3) Marjorie Thorpe
Department of English
University of the West Indies
St Augustine, Trinidad.

National Machinery for the Integration of Women in Development

Ms Lana Connor
Coordinator for Women's Affairs
Community Development
  Department
The Valley
ANGUILLA

Ms Cora Bain
Ministry of Labour, Youth, Sports
  and Community Affairs
PO Box 10014
Nassau
BAHAMAS

Ms Gwendolyn Tonge
Director
Women's Desk
Ministry of Education
St John's
ANTIGUA

Ms Joan Williams
Director
Department of Women's Affairs
Ministry of Information and Culture
Culloden Farm, Culloden Road
St Michael, BARBADOS

Ms Pat Sinclair
Director
Women's Bureau
Ministry of Youth and Community
    Development
61 Half Way Tree Road
Kingston 10
JAMAICA

Ms Constance Mitcham
Minister for Women's Affairs
Basseterre
ST KITTS

Ms Millicent Bass
Chief Community Development
    Officer
Ministry of Education, Health and
    Community Services
Plymouth
MONTSERRAT

Ms Dorla Bowman
Director
Women's Bureau
Ministry of Labour, Social Services
    and Community Development
44 Gabourel Lane
PO Box 846
Belize City
BELIZE

Ms Hyacinth Elwin
Director
Women's Desk
Ministry of Home Affairs
Roseau
DOMINICA

Ms Margaret Neckles
The Director
Women's Affairs
Ministry of Community
    Development
St George's
GRENADA

The Director
Women's Affairs Bureau
Prime Minister's Office
237 Camp Street
Cummingsburg
Georgetown
GUYANA

Sr Community Development Officer
Ministry of Social Affairs
Castries
ST LUCIA

Mrs Yvonne Francis-Gibson
The Coordinator
Women's Bureau
Ministry of Information and
    Women's Affairs
Kingstown
ST VINCENT

Ms Phyllis Augustus
Secretary
National Commission on Status
    of Women
Riverside Plaza
Besson and Picadilly Streets
Port of Spain
TRINIDAD

Appendix 2: Resource Material on Caribbean Women

Books, Articles, Papers, Reports, etc.

Antrobus, Peggy, *Strategies for Promoting the Integration of Women in Development* (Barbados, WAND, 1979).

——, *Assessment of Education and Action Programmes for Rural Women: Report on the Windward Islands* (Barbados, WAND, 1981).

——, *The Relationship between Governmental and Non-Governmental Organisations in Women in Development Programmes in the Caribbean* (1981).

——, *Assessment of Education and Action Programmes for Rural Women: Report on the Windward Islands* (Barbados, WAND, 1981).

——, *Equality, Development and Peace: a Second Look at the Goals of the UN Decade for Women* (Barbados, WAND, 1983).

——, *Women in Development within the Regional Agricultural Extension Project* (Barbados, WAND, 1983).

——, *Development* (Barbados, WAND, 1984).

——, *Human Development: New Approaches and Applications* (Barbados, WAND, 1984).

Bell, Jeanette, *Report on Antigua Small Business Management Workshop* (Barbados, WAND, 1983).

——, *Report on the Training Workshop for the Staff of CWTC* (St Vincent, 1983).

——, *Report on St Kitts Small Business Management Workshop Focusing on Financial Management* (1984).

——, *Report on St Vincent Small Business Management Workshop Focusing on Record-keeping* (Barbados, WAND, 1984).

——, *Report: Background of Nevis IRDP* (restricted) (Barbados. WAND, 1984).

——, *Women in the Caribbean: Facts Sheet* (Barbados, WAND, 1985).

——, *The Workshop of the Montserrat National Organisation of Women* (Barbados, WAND, 1985).

——, *Workshop Report on the Status of Women in Montserratian Society and the Role of National Machinery* (Barbados, WAND, 1984).

Bird, Edris, *The Influence and Involvement of Women in Formal and Non-Formal Education in the Caribbean*: a paper presented at the Caribbean Regional Council for Adult Education (Bahamas, Adult Education Association, 1983).

Bishop, Myrtle D., *Employment of Women in Dominica and Trinidad & Tobago* (Guyana, Caribbean Community Secretariat, 1984).

Blackwood, Florette, *Unemployment—A Symptom of Social Attitudes* (Jamaica,

Women's Bureau, 1980).

Broder, Erna, *Perceptions of Caribbean Women* (Barbados, ISER, 1982).

Campbell, Versada, S., *Health and Nutrition of Women Engaged in Marketing Agricultural Produce in Parochial Markets* (Jamaica, CFNI, 1984).

Carasco, Beryl et al., *The Impact of Rural Development Schemes on Low-Income Households and the Role of Women* (Barbados, WAND, 1983).

——, *Women in Agriculture and Rural Development* (Barbados, WAND, 1983).

Caribbean Resource Book compiled by the Bureau of Jamaica, Extra-Mural Department (New York), International Women's Tribune Centre, 1979).

Caribbean Resource Kit for Women (Barbados, WAND, IWTC, 1982).

CFPA, *Guidance and Teenage Counselling in Family Life and Teenage Sexuality* (Montserrat, UWI, 1982).

CFPA, *Methods of Teaching Family Life Education in the Classroom* (Antigua, UWI, 1982).

CFPA, *Teaching Human Sexuality in Caribbean Schools, a Teacher's Handbook* (NY, IPPF, 1982).

Creating a "Woman's Component": A case study in Rural Jamaica (Washington, WID, 1980).

Cole, Joyce, *Women and Education*, vol.5 (Barbados, ISER, 1982).

Craig, Christine, *Everything but the Ring* (Jamaica, Bureau of Women's Affairs, 1982).

Cropper, Angela, *The Integration of Women in Development: Fact sheet for the Caribbean (Windward & Leeward Islands)* (Barbados, WAND, 1980).

——, *The Integration of Women in Development for Windward and Leeward Islands of the Caribbean: a situation study* (Barbados, WAND, 1980).

Cumper, Gloria & Stephanie Daley, *Family Law in the Commonwealth Caribbean* (Mona, UWI, 1979).

Cumper, Gloria, *Survey of Social Legislation in Jamaica* (Jamaica, ISER, 1972).

Cuthbert, Marlene, *The Impact of Cultural Industries in the Field of Audio-Visual Media on the Socio-Cultural Behaviour of Women in Jamaica* (Jamaica, UWI, 1979).

Cuthbert, Marlene (ed.), *Women and Media Decision-making in the Caribbean* (Jamaica, CARIMAC/UNESCO Seminar, 1981).

Daly, Stephanie, *The Developing Legal Status of Women in Trinidad & Tobago* (Trinidad & Tobago, National Commission on the Status of Women, 1982).

Dixon, Mary, *A New Dawn for Women* (Jamaica, Jamal Foundation, 1975).

Donawa, Wendy, *Women's Studies—Lesson Outlines for Course at Barbados Community College* (1984).

Duncan, Neville & Kenneth O'Brien, *Women and Politics in Barbados 1948-1981*, vol.3 (Barbados, ISER, 1983).

Durrant-Gonzales, Victoria, *Women and the Family*, vol.2 (Barbados, ISER, 1982).

Ellis, Pat, *Adult Education, Training and Employment "Beyond Rhetoric— The Focus on Women"* (Barbados, WAND, 1981).

——, *Mini Courses in Social Studies: An Introduction to Women's Studies Prepared for Social Studies Education* (Barbados, WAND, 1981).

——, *Pilot Project for the Integration of Women in Rural Development —St. Vincent.* (Barbados, WAND, 1981).

——, *Pilot Project for the Integration of Women in Rural Development— St Vincent: A case study on non-formal education* (Barbados, WAND, 1981).

——, *Getting the Community into the Act: a training manual of participatory*

activities for fieldworkers (Barbados, WAND, 1983).
————, *The Participation of Women in the Caribbean Association of Peasants and Agricultural Workers* (Barbados, WAND, 1982).
————, *Teachers and Sex-Role Stereotyping they Contribute—they Can Help to Correct It!* (Barbados, WAND, 1982).
————, *Women and Adult Non-Formal Education: the Use of Participatory Methods in a Community-Based Adult Education Programme* (Barbados, WAND, 1982).
————, *From Silent Beneficiaries to Active Participants and Contributors to the Development Process* (Barbados, WAND, 1983).
————, *Pilot Project as a Strategy for Influencing Policy* (Barbados, WAND, 1983).
————, *The Role of Women in Rural Development—The Rose Hall Experience: Bottom-Up Development in Action* (Barbados, WAND, 1983).
————, *Sisterhood and Solidarity—A Strategy for Providing Services and Support for Women* (Barbados, WAND, 1983).
Ellis, Pat and Lionel Egbert, *Of Confrontation and Change: Women and Men in Development* (a workshop report on the role of men in the development of Rose Hall, St Vincent), (Barbados, WAND, 1983).
Forde, Norma, *Women and the Law*, vol.1 (Barbados, ISER, 1981).
Gill, Margaret, *Women Work and Development* (Barbados, ISER, 1981).
Gordon-Gofton, Lorna, *Women and Media: Decision making in the Caribbean* (Jamaica, CARIMAC/UNESCO, 1981).
Gussler, Judith D., *Adaptive Strategies and Social Networks of Women in St Kitts* (NY, PSS, 1980).
Hamilton, Jill, *Women of Barbados: Amerindian era to mid-20th Century* (Barbados, Letchworth Press.)
Hamilton, Marlene, *The Evidence of Sex-Typed Behaviours in Professional Jamaican Men and Women* (Jamaica, School of Education, 1981).
————, *Professional Jamaican Women—Equal Or Not?* (UWI, School of Education, 1980).
Hamilton, Marlene and Leo-Rhynie, Elsa, *Sex-Role Stereotyping and Education—the Jamaican Perspective* (Jamaica, UWI, School of Education, 1979).
Henry, Francis and Wilson, Pamela, 'The Status of Women in Caribbean Societies: An Overview of their Social, Economic and Sexual Roles' (*Social and Economic Studies*, vol.24, No. 2, 1975).
Hope, Margaret, *Journey in the Shaping: Report of the first symposium on Women in Caribbean Culture* (Barbados, WAND, 1983).
ISER, *Women in the Caribbean Project and Health* (Barbados, ISER, 1982).
Jagdeo, Tirbani, P., *Adolescent Pregnancy in the Caribbean: Context, Causes and Consequences* (Antigua, CFPA, 1982).
————, *Teenage Pregnancy in the Caribbean* (NY, IPPF, 1984).
Johnson, Catherine 'Leah', *The Role of Communication in the Development of the Caribbean* (special focus on women) (Montserrat, Research paper, 1980).
Knudson, Barbara, *The Economic Role of Women in Small-Scale Agriculture in the Caribbean: St Lucia and St Vincent compared* (University of Minnesota, July, 1982 (draft)).
Massiah, Joycelin, *Employed Women in Barbados: a Demographic Profile, 1946-1970* (Barbados, ISER, 1984).
————, *Female-Headed Households and Development in the Caribbean* (Barbados, ISER, 1981).

———, *Women as Heads of Households in the Caribbean: Family Structure and Feminine Status* (UK, UNESCO, 1983).

Mathurin, Lucille, *The Rebel Woman in the British West Indies during Slavery* (Jamaica, Institute of Jamaica for the African Caribbean, 1975).

Mordecai, Pamela & Mervyn Morris (eds), *Jamaican Woman: an Anthology of Poems* (Trinidad, Heinemann, 1980).

Paper On Legal Status of Women—Dominica, compiled and presented by Ismanie Royer (Dominica, Bureau, 1983).

Planning For Women In Rural Development: a Source Book for the Caribbean (Barbados, WAND, NY Pop. Council, 1984).

Pitts, Cynthia, *Women and their Citizenship in Jamaica* (Jamaica, Norman Manley Law School, 1975).

The Population Council, *Female Workers Undercounted: the Case of Latin America and Caribbean Censuses* (Mexico, Population Council, 1982).

Reddock, Rhoda, *Clotil Walcott and the Struggle of the Trinidad & Tobago Working Class Woman* (Trinidad).

Report of the Meeting to Discuss Project to Promote Desirable Attitudal Changes in Men and Women to help Achieve the Goals of the UN Decade for Women (Chairperson Ms M. Pollard, Women's Affairs Officer CARICOM Secretariat) (Guyana, Caribbean Community Secretariat, 1982).

The Report of the National Commission on the Status of Women in Barbados, vols. I & II (Government of Barbados, 1978).

Roberts, George W. and Sonja A., *Women in Jamaica: Patterns of Reproduction and Family* (USA, Kraus Thompson, 1978).

Shorey-Bryan, Norma, *Male/Female Socialization, Career Counselling and Jobs for Women and Men* (Barbados, WAND, 1983).

———, *Training Sessions Conducted Within Fieldworkers and Staff of Social League* (Barbados, WAND, 1982).

St. Cyr, Joaquin, *Women as the Recipients of Services from Resources Allocated in the National Budget of Trinidad and Tobago* (ECLA/CARIB, 1983).

Simon, Patricia, *The Law Relating to Women in Antigua, Bahamas, Belize, Cayman Islands, Dominica, Trinidad & Tobago* (1980).

WAND, *Caribbean Women and their Participation in Economic, Political and Social Development* (Barbados, WAND, 1979).

Women's Affair's Bureau, *Overview of the Status of Women in Guyana* (Guyana, Bureau, 1983).

Women's Affairs Bureau, *Report on National Seminar on "The Role and Functions of the Women's Affair's Bureau in Guyana", Linkages at the National Regional and International Level* (Guyana, Women's Affairs Bureau, 1983).

Women in the Informal Sector with Special Reference to Street Foods (Jamaica, CFNI, 1984).

Wyre, V. Iothie, *A Study of the Occupation of the Rural Jamaican Market Woman* (Jamaica, UWI, 1975).

Newsletters, Journals, Bulletins etc.

WAND houses a collection of over a hundred different titles of newsletters, journals, bulletins and papers dealing with issues concerning women in development. A selection of this material includes:

Caribbean Women's Features Syndicate (CWFS) (Barbados, WAND, 1983).
CARICOM Perspective (Guyana, CARICOM Secretariat, 1981).
Woman Speak! (Barbados, WAND, 1979).
Woman Struggle (Barbados, WAND, 1982).
Women in Struggle (Barbados, Concerned Women for Progress, 1982).*

*Issues concerning Women and Development is a continuing series of articles to stimulate discussion and debate in the Caribbean region (Barbados, WAND, 1979).

To mark the end of the Decade for Women, the Women and Development Unit (WAND) in cooperation with the Caribbean Women's Features Syndicate (CWFS) has put out a special series of Issues papers:

Anderson, Beverley, *Caribbean Women and the Political Process* (February 1985).
Peacocke, Nan, *Crimes Against Women—Women's Solidarity* (March, 1985).
Antrobus, Peggy, *Institutions and Programmes for the Decade* (March, 1985).
——, *The Issue is Peace* (February, 1985).
Shorey-Bryan, Norma, *The Status of Male/Female Relationships* (May, 1985).
Bell, Jeanette, *Women and Entrepreneurship* (April, 1985).
Clarendon, Hannah, *Women and Food Production a Waste of Productive Capacity* (April, 1985).
Durant-Gonzalez, Victoria, *Women and Industry* (March, 1985).
Ellis, Pat, *Women, Adult Education and Literacy: a Caribbean Perspective* (January 1985).

Audio-Visual Material

Slides
Caribbean Woman Advance, script by Lorna Gordon-Gofton (Barbados, WAND).
IWTC, *Caribbean Women Speak Out* (Barbados, WAND).
Issues in Caribbean Development (Commissioned by UNESCO), script by Lorna Gordon-Gofton (Barbados, WAND).
Planning for Women in Rural Development (based on the Regional Research Project on the Impact of Rural Development Schemes on low-income households and the role of women), script by Lorna Gordon-Gofton (Barbados, WAND).
Rose Hall Community Integrating Women into Rural Development, script by the women of Rose Hall with Pat Ellis and Valerie Wint-Bauer (Barbados, WAND).

Video-Tapes
The Rose Hall Experience, script by Norma Shorey-Bryan (Barbados, WAND).
Sweet Sugar Rage (statements based on ISER Research Project Women in the Caribbean), script by Lorna Gordon-Gofton (Barbados, WAND).

"Woman Time" (based on symposium Women in Culture), script by Lorna Gordon-Gofton (Barbados, WAND).

Audio Tapes

WAND houses over three hundred in a series of United Nations radio tapes (reel-to-reel) entitled *WOMEN*. These tapes cover a wide range of WID-related topics ranging from interviews, discussions, readings and verbal reports. The majority of these tapes were produced during the period 1980-1984. A selection of topics from these tapes is as follows:

Talk on traditional medicine and childbirth practices.
Discrimination against women.
Women in the labour market.
Women and the mass media.
Women in the liberation movement.
Women's Bureau in Jamaica.
Women and mental health.
Job discrimination against women.
Dame Nita Barrow talks about her work with the world-wide YWCA.
Women, energy and finance.
Women and ageing.
UN Commission on the Status of Women.
Battered women.
Family planning.
Women and modern technology.
Women in the arts.
Women in industrial planning.
Women workers' rights.

Housed also at WAND is a collection of radio tapes which deal with a wide range of topics:

The labels and reinforcement of sex-role stereotyping
Agri-business
Business management
Management of assets
Setting up your business
Manufacturing

Posters

WAND's poster series focuses on non-traditional jobs, career options, employment, non-formal education and development planning as they relate to women. Specific titles are as follows:

Expand your Horizons.
Planning for Rural Development.
Popular Education.
Women and Employment.

PAREDOS posters reflecting images of family life are also available at WAND.

Notes on Contributors

Notes on Contributors

Peggy Antrobus is Tutor Coordinator of the Women and Development Unit (WAND) of the Extra-Mural Department, University of the West Indies (UWI), Cave Hill Campus, Barbados. She was the first director of the Jamaican Women's Bureau (1974), the first national machinery for the integration of women to be established in the Caribbean, She is well known regionally and internationally for her untiring efforts and commitment to women's issues and concerns.

Jeanette Belle is a Barbadian and a field programme officer at WAND. With a background in health and sociology, she is particularly interersted in women's health and in promoting their involvement in small business enterprises. She has been working with women in the Eastern Caribbean to help them to develop their skills and improve their capabilities in this area.

Beryl Carasco is a St Lucian with wide experience in the field of secondary and adult education. She has worked on women's affairs at national and regional levels and has done research on various aspects of women's issues. A free-lance consultant in research, project evaluation and training, she is currently on assignment to the Caribbean Conference of Churches.

Hannah Clarendon is a Dominican, a plant pathologist who works as a crop protection officer in the Ministry of Agriculture. She has worked extensively with the local hucksters and was instrumental in helping them to organize the Dominica Hucksters Association, the first in the region. She has done a lot of research on women in agriculture in Dominica.

Claudette Earle is a Guyanese journalist who is editor of the *Guyana Chronicle*, the national newspaper. She is a correspondent for the Caribbean Women's Features Syndicate.

Honor Ford-Smith is a Jamaican and a tutor at the Jamaica School of Drama. She is artistic director of Sistren Collective. She has done considerable research on women's struggles in a historical perspective in Jamaica and is actively engaged with Sistren in using these research findings to develop and disseminate print and audio-visual material to raise consciousness on women's issues.

Barbara Gloudon is a Jamaican journalist and communications consultant, who manages her own consulting firm. She is also a playwright and has written many of the scripts used in the annual pantomime, as social commentary on the Jamaican situation.

Lorna Gordon is a Jamaican journalist and communications consultant with seventeen years' experience in printing and broadcasting in Jamaica. She now owns and operates her own consulting company. She is coordinator of the Caribbean Women's Features Syndicate, has written widely on women's issues and has developed and produced materials for women and development activities in the region.

Angela Hammel-Smith is a Trinidadian. Previously a secondary school teacher at St. Joseph Convent Port of Spain, she was shop steward and was actively involved in the formation of the Trinidad and Tobago United Teachers Association. She is now employed as an Industrial Relations Manager with The National Petroleum Company.

Sonia Harris is a Jamaican who is a consultant for the Social Development Institute in Jamaica. She has extensive experience in working with women, both at the national level in the government national planning agency and the Women's Bureau and at the community level. She has done considerable research into the lives of poor rural and urban women in Jamaica.

Annette Isaac is a Trinidadian living in Ottawa. A consultant in International Development, she is particularly concerned about how the work of International Development Agencies affect the lives, and the social and economic status of women in developing countries especially in the Caribbean. She has provided consultancy services to CIDA on their WID programme in the Caribbean and has her own consultancy firm.

Stephanie Kamugisha is a Barbadian journalist trained in Canada who has worked for the Government Information Service in Barbados for three years and now teaches adults part-time. She has lived in Tanzania where she worked as Executive Officer in charge of publications at the Institute of Development Management in Dar es Salaam.

Patricia Mohammed is a Trinidadian and a Research Associate at the Institute of Social and Economic Research, University of the West Indies, Trinidad. She co-tutored the first course on Research on Women and Men in Development organized by the Institute of Development Studies, University of Sussex, England in 1984. She is coordinator of the recently opened (first) Rape Crisis Centre in Port-of-Spain. She is actively involved in a number of women's groups locally and regionally.

Elma Reyes is a Trinidadian and a free-lance journalist. One of the first, she writes widely for the local (Trinidadian) as well as for the regional press. She is a correspondent for the Caribbean Women Features Syndicate.

Rhodda Reddock is a Trinidadian and research fellow at the Institute of Social and Economic Research, University of the West Indies, Trinidad. She taught for three years on the Master's programme in Women and Development Studies at the Institute of Social Studies, The Hague, from which she recently received her doctorate. Her doctoral dissertation is *Women, Labour and Struggle in Trinidad and Tobago 1898-1960.*

Norma Shorey-Bryan is a Barbadian, currently Programme Coordinator at WAND. She is particularly interested in the issue of how boys and girls are socialized. She has conducted a number of training activities aimed at raising the awareness of parents, teachers, young people and employers about the implications of this issue for male-female relationships in the Caribbean.

Rosalind Saint Victor is a Trinidadian who is coordinator of the Caribbean Family Planning Affiliation in Antigua. She has had extensive experience in education and counselling both in North America and the Caribbean and is particularly interested in family life-education and human sexuality.

Cheryl Williams is a Trinidadian teaching English at the Arima Senior Comprehensive School. She is particularly interested in the many traditional indigenous cultural forms that have influenced and shaped Caribbean cultural identity. She has done research on how the process of development and urbanization have affected these cultural forms, and has been influenced by them in their turn.